THE IMAGE OF MODERN MAN IN T. S. ELIOT'S POETRY

THE IMAGE OF MODERN MAN IN T. S. ELIOT'S POETRY

Mariwan Nasradeen Hasan Barzinji

authorHOUSE®

AuthorHouse™
1663 Liberty Drive
Bloomington, IN 47403
www.authorhouse.com
Phone: 1-800-839-8640

Published by AuthorHouse   11/16/2012

ISBN: 978-1-4772-4704-4 (sc)
ISBN: 978-1-4772-4705-1 (e)

DEDICATED TO:

The teacher of humanity (Prophet Muhammad)
peace and blessings of Allah be upon him.

All my teachers in the past, present and future.

ABSTRACT

This book "The Image of the Modern Man in Selected Poems of T.S. Eliot" attempts to portray the image of the modern man in a selection of Eliot's famous poems. Critics have hinted at this image in his poems but few have attempted to highlight it chronologically in detail. This study also examines all the aspects of the modern man's life. Reader response analysis approach is used while analysing the poems.

The first chapter, the "Introduction" attempts to define the image of the modern man as it came into use by the modern poets then, certain non-literary and literary factors and influences, which shaped the modern poetry and modern society, are discussed and Eliot's role as a modern poet and representative of modernity is highlighted. Finally, the technique that Eliot used to depict the image of the modern man is pinpointed.

The second chapter "Prufrock as a Representative of Modern Man in *The Love Song of J. Alfred Prufrock*" (1917) tackles the modern man as inactive, shy and impotent being incapable of solving his problems. Prufrock, who may be Eliot himself, represents the modern man. The poet ascribes these problems to the modern man himself who has lost faith in God, which resulted from the destructive effects of the First World War.

The third chapter "Tiresias as a Modern Man in *The Waste Land*" (1922) presents the same image of the modern man as sterile like the Fisher King. Eliot presents some characters in the poem to indicate that the modern man lives in a chaotic and disorderly life, because he has neglected God and has immersed himself in the materialistic world.

Chapter Four consists of three parts; the first part is "the image of the modern man in *The Hollow Men*" (1925), where Eliot depicts the modern man as hollow. In this poem, the modern man realises his hollowness; therefore, he wants to repent for the sins that he has committed. The poet highlights that the modern man is soon subject of despair since he is spiritually empty. This poem also shows Eliot's life; when he was writing the poem, he was prepared to be baptised and purified from his sins. The modern man, who has realised his sins, repents and finally returns to God. The second part includes: "The Image of the Modern Man in *Ash-Wednesday*" (1927), which deals with the modern man and his turning to religion. The poet has confirmed that by the modern man's returning to God, the modern man will have a meaningful life, then the poet alludes to the Virgin as an intercessor for the modern man, which means the poet as the representative of modern man is hopeful because he has finally reached the end of his journey, which starts in his *The Love Song of J. Alfred Prufrock* and ends in his *Four Quartets*. The last part of the study is the conclusion section which sums up the findings of the study and infers that Eliot was a pioneer among the poets in vividly delineating the image of the modern man through studying the psychic, mental, emotional and social states, which was prevailed during a specific period in the life of people in his own community.

CONTENTS

CHAPTER ONE

Introduction

Thomas Parkinson states that the modern man is a term, which is invented by modern poetry to dignify modern people's skepticism (Parkinson, 1951: 5). Eliot has depicted the image of modern man in his poems to reflect their problems in the entire world.

Before considering modern poetry, something should be said about the modern temper; i.e., about certain non-literary influences shaping the modern poetry and the audience who received it and gave it its fame. Shakti Batra in his book *T.S. Eliot: A Critical Study of his Poetry,* points out two important factors that left great influence on modern poetry: first, the audience in the twentieth century has been, to an unprecedented degree, interested in mental phenomena by introspection. The growing prestige of psychology as a subject of investigation has been paralleled in prose literature by the works of such writers as Joyce and Proust. Each of them creates enormous verbal fabrics out of the development and history of a single sensibility. The second factor is the modern temper which by contrast with the Victorian temper, has been characterized by more anxiety and insecurity than by confidence and assurance (Batra, 2001: 2).

In a spiritual sense, the period induced insecurity by its revolt against traditions of all kinds. This revolt led to political uncertainty. It has been said that a large number of conversions and apostasies were experienced by modern intellectual leaders in the twentieth century. The spread of doubts is also seen in the twentieth century about human freedom and human dignity. Determinism and Marxism were two of the new ideologies brought by Sigmund Freud (1856-1939), and Carl Marx (1818-1883). Freud had suggested that human individuals are predetermined by formation or malformation of the unconscious parts of their minds during infancy or early childhood but Marxism had suggested that human societies, in their organization and historical development, are predetermined by economic or technological considerations (Kaplan, 2006: 5).

The most controversial aspect of the modern movement was its rejection of tradition. Modernism's stress on freedom of expression, experimentation, radicalism, and primitivism disregards conventional expectations. In many forms of art, that controversy over the rejection of tradition often meant startling and alienating audiences with bizarre and unpredictable effects, the strange and disturbing combinations of motifs in Surrealism, and the use of extreme dissonance and atonality in modernist music. The technique of modern literature is often involved in the rejection of intelligible plots or characterization in novels, or the invention in poetry that rejected clear interpretation. The Soviet Communist government rejected modernism after the rise of Stalin on the grounds of alleged elitism, although it had previously gave approval to Futurism and Constructivism, and the Nazi government in Germany considered it narcissistic and ridiculous (Berghaus, 2000: 212). The Nazis exhibited modernist paintings alongside with works which were considered the mentally ill in an exhibition entitled *Degenerate Art*. In fact, modernism flourished mainly in consumer/capitalist societies, despite the fact that its proponents often rejected consumerism itself. However, high modernism began to merge with consumer culture after World War II, especially during the 1960s. The likes of Bob Dylan, Serge Gainsbourg and *The Rolling Stones* combined popular musical traditions with modernist verse, adopting literary devices derived from James Joyce, Samuel Beckett, James Thurber, T. S. Eliot, Guillaume Apollinaire, Allen Ginsberg, and others. Modernist design also began to enter the mainstream of popular culture, as simplified and stylized forms, which were often associated with dreams of a space age high-tech future that became popular. This merging of consumer and high versions of modernist culture resulted in a radical transformation of the meaning of "modernism" (Grant, 1999: 100). Firstly, it implied that a movement based on the rejection of tradition had become a tradition of its own, and secondly, it demonstrated that the distinction between elite modernist and mass consumerist culture had lost its quality of being precise. Some writers declared that modernism had become institutionalized, and in some other fields, the effects of modernism have remained the strongest.

Modern poetry is known as being very unusual, and obscure. The heart of this vagueness mirrors the complexity of the modern life and its problems because poetry has been a medium for reflecting the entire problems of modern man. The problems are artistically reflected in the poetry of T.S. Eliot. Eliot's poetry is similar to the metaphysical poetry because he, like the metaphysical poets, uses conventional images in a startling way and creates new images by using unexpected literary devices like, metaphor, and juxtaposition and linked very far-fetched ideas in his poetry. For instance, in *The Love of Song of J. Alfred Prufrock*, the opening simile of "the patient etherized upon a table" sets the tone for the images, which follow in the poem (Thorne, 2006:289).

Modern poetry dramatizes the problems of the modern age, which permeates experience in terms of values, ethics, social and psychological problems. Modern poets are different from the romantic poets, who tried to find solutions for individual's problems. However, modern poets seek to understand this split of modern man in a modern way. The sense of incompleteness, alienation and that of irrecoverable loss of existence without spiritual centre has nowhere been cleverly dramatized than in *The Hollow Men* (Shakti, Batra, 2001: 3-5).

English and American modern poetry had several independent voices that question contemporary important events and catastrophes of the age. The most important aspect of modern poetry is the special way of perceiving life and dealing with the world, because of the radical changes brought about by the first and second world wars. The destructive results of these two wars led to the creation of a new type of poetry, which was quite different from the poetry before the war in content and style, i.e., the poetry of the Victorian age at the late nineteenth century and the early beginning of the twentieth century. The devastating results of World War I caused a change in many European countries and brought about radical changes in the social life and disillusionment among people. The great losses faced by a large number of people in different countries changed the way people perceived religion, tradition and ethics, which created a shake in their beliefs and even in their political ideologies. Theologians, public intellectuals, and academicians argued that the forces of modernization were so powerful that they inevitably secularized western society and rendered religious belief old-fashioned. Churches and religious movements were doomed to extinction. But Balmar, in his book, *Religion in Twentieth Century America,* states, nothing could be far from the truth. "Instead of dying, religion has thrived as never before. Whether measured by church attendance rates, national opinion polls, or charitable activities, this nation, arguably the most modern in the world, is also the most religious." (Balmar, 2001: 7)

The poetry of the age mirrors the new social, religious and political changes in the life of the people and their disillusionment. World War I was a very sad and catastrophic experience for the entire European countries and of the world in general, but its impact was much greater on the intellectual people. (Batra, 2001: 3-5). It was after that destructive war that some modern poets like Eliot brought a new way of writing poetry "In defining themselves as innovative, Eliot and Pound rejected much Victorian literature for its out-moded Romanticism" (Cronin etal, 2002: 513).

Tiwari states that Cleanth Brook points out that Eliot, like John Donne, belonged to the tradition of wit and paradox in English poetry. In his poetry, Eliot has portrayed the atmosphere of crime and the horror faced by humanity in the modern societies. Eliot has used the Greek myth in his poetry because he, like the symbolists, found a very deep spirituality in Greek mythology, which was quite different from the vulgarity of the modern world surrounding them. Eliot and the symbolist poets tried to present a picture of the ideal life in contrast to the debasement of values of the world in which modern man lives (Tiwari, 2001:1-3).

It is clear that Eliot knew when and why he decided to become a poet. He became a poet at the age of fourteen in 1902, after he read a copy of Fitz Gerard's free translation of *The Rubáiyát of Omar Khayyam,* which had left an impact on his imagination (Jr. Miller, 2005:2). In the winter of 1910-1911, when Eliot was studying in Paris, he read three of Dostoevsky's novels *Crime and Punishment, The idiot* and *The Brothers Karamazov,* on which he comments that "These three novels made a very profound impression on me and I had read them all before Prufrock was completed" (Southam, 1968: 18).

The poetry of Eliot, on the one hand, shows the catastrophes faced by modern man, like alienation, and on the other hand, suggests the solution for each single problem. Lewis Feuer argues that the problem of modern man is not specifically modern, it is omnipresent. "What stands out from a historical and comparative standpoint is the omnipresence of alienation; it takes different guises in all societies" (Feuer, 1969, 90).

It is said that the lack of basic wisdom is one of the salient characteristics of Eliot's poetry. Eliot's poetic revolution was complex in its effects. In fact, he introduced the urban element into his work as an essential and vital change in poetry; but Eliot's imitators gave the readers the notion that his poetry is obscure without the essential vision and wisdom that underlie the originality and made a virtue out of incomprehensibility (Stephen Martin, 1984: 97).

Marlowe. A. Miller in his book, *Masterpieces of British Modernism* states that Virginia Woolf has declared that human nature, and human relations changed at about 1910. This change included master-slave relationship and that of the family members; especially between the parents and their children (Miller, 2006: 1). Any change in the human nature results in changes in viewing religion, conduct and most of the aspects of life. Woolf's comment refers to those radical changes in those aspects of the modern society, which paved the way for the new poetry in many countries like America and the United Kingdom.

T.S. Eliot has been accused of "obscurity and pretentiousness" (Southam, 1974:15). Eliot touched the question of difficulty in modern poetry. He said that difficulty is not something peculiar to certain writers but a condition of writing in the contemporary world. In a context of "great variety and complexity", the modern poet can only respond with "various and complex results": "The poet must become more and more comprehensive, more allusive, more indirect to force, to dislocate if necessary, language into his meaning." Much of Eliot's poetry can be read with pleasure at the first sight, although it might not be fully grasped; Eliot points out in this regard saying: "I know that some of the poetry to which I am most devoted is poetry to which I did not understand at first reading", and also insists that when poetry calls for knowledge, the poetry-lover must be prepared to answer the demand (Southam, 1974:16).

A factor that obstructed the development of American poetry was the vast distances among the poets who showed some talent, and may have thrived in a center, which did not allow them communicate with one another. On the contrary, London was that center where the writers could meet and communicate, but the United States saw no movement at the end of the century like the 1890s poets in London who rebelled against the Victorian moralities and the late nineteenth-century version of Romanticism. Outside the Harvard and New York centers, American poets worked alone to educate themselves by benefiting from the anthologies of English poetry. Frustration with the cultural climate of the United States had already, by the turn of the century, led to the mass exodus to Europe, of the painters, like Whistler(1834-1903) and Mary Cassatt (1844-1926), and the writers like Henry James (1843-1916), Gertrude Stein (1874-1946), then Pound (1885-1972), <u>Hilda Doolittle (1886-1961)</u>, and T. S. Eliot (1888-1965), and later in 1920s to a generation of expatriates, including Ernest Hemingway (1899-1961) and F. Scott Fitzgerald (1896-1940), (MacGown, 2004: 11).

1910 was the year King Edward VII died and the year that woman's demands to obtain the vote (suffrage) gained momentum and met violent police retaliation.1910 was also the final year of the dominance of the Liberal Party over England. Whether one accepts the date (1910) suggested by Woolf or not, it is obvious that modernists occupied the first forty years of the twentieth century. (Miller, 2006:1). Virginia Woolf links the changes, which occurred in the twentieth century, to the radical shift in the modern world caused by World War I. In "How It Strikes a Contemporary" written in 1923, Woolf states "we are sharply cut off from our predecessors. A shift in the scale—the war, the sudden slip of masses held in position for ages—has shaken the fabric from top to bottom, alienated us from the past" (The Essays, Vol. 4, 238). For speaking of the aims of the modern poets, Henderson and Monroe quoted Mr. Yeats's speech, who states that,

> We were weary of the art of Tennyson and his imitators. We wanted to get rid not only of rhetoric but also of poetic diction. We tried to strip away everything that was artificial, to get a style like speech, as simple as the simplest prose, like a cry of the heart (Henderson and Monroe, 1917: I X).

This was a much more serious challenge for the modern poets against the Victorians (Kreizenbec, 2004: 29). Eliot, who was against the romantic poets, wrote, "the decay of these poets mostly depends on their too much self. For a great artist, an awareness of the world outside of himself is necessary, his personal of the consciousness of the general humanity." Eliot supports the Aristotelian notion that poetry is the philosophy of writing. Its object is truth, not individual or local but general operative. In the writing of a serious poem, the poet has to be too responsible in revealing the truth; which must not be harmed by fantasies (Rao, 1996: 21). "Eliot's history is static, though tradition shows modifications" Rampal points out that Eliot in his essay *Tradition and the Individual Talent*, declares that poets are required to be aware of the whole literature of Europe since it mirrors the history and the traditions of Europe and via their awareness they can enrich their poetry (Rampal, 1996: 88). Eliot believes that a writer must develop consciousness of the past and he should try hard to develop his consciousness throughout his career. Eliot believes that the modern poets have enhanced their writings on the tradition, and it needs not to be accepted by the society (Rampal, 1996: 77). What makes Eliot one of the most famous modern writers is his derivation of his concept of time from diverse sources, which he had shaped into the theory of history and tradition.

The poet must not be only inspired but also calculative, thoughtful and responsible. Eliot further argues that,

> It is essential to establish a vital connection between the individual and the race. The struggle in art is to make the poet aware of the mind of the Europe. A mind is important which leaves in time to be more important than his own private mind (Eliot's Sacred Wood).

The very early years of the twentieth century witnessed the rebirth and transformation of poetry. Like the novelists, the poets wished to renew their art and tried to keep a distance from the stagnant condition of late Victorian literature. One of the pioneers of the modern poetry is W.B.Yeats (1865-1939) who strived to leave the conventions of the Victorian period and in the second decade of the twentieth century, Yeats was able to move away from the Celtic myths and legends that dominated his early works and used the contemporary political and social issues directly in his poetry. Gilles and Mahood state that, the vibrancy of the poetry in this period is remarkable, with a wide range of poetic movements emerging; each contested the others' aesthetics, through the various manifestos that they produced and published little magazines, many of which were founded and run by the poets themselves (Gillies and Mahood, 2007: 64-65).

There are some misunderstandings among the critics concerning Eliot's poetry. In 1931, Eliot stated that when he wrote *The Waste Land* some of the critics said that he had expressed the "disillusionment of a generation", which "is nonsense". Eliot commented that he may express modern man's own illusion of being disillusioned, but this was not part of Eliot's intension (Sandra, 1999: 530-531). Part of what is said concerning Eliot's poetry is not deniable because he is a very sensitive poet who has written about his own psychological problems and since he lived in the same society he may have similar problems with the other people because of the two destructive World Wars, which destroyed modern society. But the other part of what the critics said concerning Eliot's poetry is not believable because Eliot himself denied that and declared that he wrote his poems for himself. It can be said that Eliot's problems are like the problems of modern man, in this sense via Eliot's problems one can recognize the problems of the modern man; furthermore, Eliot is the representative of modern man that can express his sense of alienation, failure of communication as well as lack of confidence.

Ezra Pound is one of those who had left a very great influence on Eliot; when he, for the first time, showed Pound his poem *The Love Song of J. Alfred Prufrock,* he declared "he had found an American poet who had actually trained himself and modernized himself on his own" (Sandra, 1999:532). Pound's statement indicates that Eliot was not an ordinary poet. It also indicates that Eliot has enhanced his own poetry by depending on his efforts wherever he was. When a person leaves his country and joins another country his life becomes complicated and he may even give up his writing though life for Eliot became very difficult but he did not give up writing poetry but also made the quality of his work better if compared to his previous works.

Eliot's death, on January 4, 1965, at the age of seventy-six, marked the end of a bright period in English literary history. Twentieth century is the period when Eliot was the pathfinder for the other poets during his time (Batra, 2001:1). The appeal of his genius was not limited only to the English-speaking people or to the European tradition. Thus, one can say that Eliot is English, a European and a universal poet because of his influence on world literature of the twentieth century, and has been one of the great dominant forces in English literature of the twentieth century. If any reader wants to understand Eliot's poetry, he should read the whole body of his writing, not only his poetic and dramatic productions but also his religious and cultural criticism as well as his editorial works at the British publishing house (Faber and Faber). One can see his role in the modern world in general and in modern poetry in particular (Damrosch and Dettmar, 2006: 2506).

In his book *T.S. Eliot's Major Poems and Plays*, Kaplan says:

> No single poet has influenced the development of modern American poetry quite as much as T.S. Eliot, both as poet and critic. His serious publication appeared in 1915; Henry James (1843-1916) was still alive; indeed, Emerson and Longfellow had died only some thirty years earlier, and Whitman, Wittier and Holmes only some twenty years earlier. Eliot is roughly contemporary with the generation of Edwin Arlington Robinson, Robert Frost, Carl Standburg, Vachel Lindsay, Willa Cather, H. L. Mencken, Sinclair Lewis, and Robison Jeffers (Kaplan, 1997: 5).

This shows that Eliot was one of the earliest modern poets. His coming in the beginning of the twentieth century is startling, for Eliot's poetry was as different from the poetry of the nineteenth century as it was different from that of the fifteenth century. There are many literary figures by which Eliot was influenced like, Byron, Bergson, Babbitt, as well as the French symbolists. Eliot combined these influences with the pessimistic view of modern man and used them in his poetry and the critical works, which have largely shaped the English and American modern poetry. Dwivedi confirms the same argument, and points out that the role of the American poets of the twentieth century cannot be neglected. In his book entitled *T. S. Eliot, The Critical Study*, Dwivedi points out that Eliot was not only a poet but also a critic and a playwright and highlights that "Eliot's images are drawn directly from life or his own experiences and knowledge. They are an integral part of his eventful life." (Dwivedi, 2002: 35).

Eliot's role as a literary figure was prominent, and his influence is obviously seen in many fields like poetry, drama and literary criticism, religious and social thought. "However, his importance as a critic and as a religious and social thinker was and still is felt in so diffused and oblique a manner that it seemed fitting to confine the area of interest to his poetry and plays" (Grant, 1982: 1). Yeats' comment on T.S. Eliot, in his introduction to *The Oxford Book of Modern Verse* suggests an intimate understanding of the ethos of a religious person. He says: "Eliot's religion compared to that of John Gray, Francis Thomson, Lionel Johnson in *The Dark Angel* lacks all strong emotion; a New England Protestant by decent, there is little self-surrender in his personal relation to God and the soul" (Yeats. W.B, OBMV1975: XXII).

The sense of failure, which Eliot has expressed in a psychological symbolism, is derived from Freud, and to some degree from Jung. Eliot mixes the technique of "free verse" with the colloquial conversation which echoes his sense of kinship with the juxtapositions of the past and the present time, to reflect both his philosophical concern with the modern time, and his belief in the past as important in terms of meaningful ritual and tradition.

It is probably this latter conviction, which led him to give up "young" America for the older civilization of England and the old rituals of the Church of England. In his introduction to *For Lancelot Andrews*, Eliot describes himself as "an Anglo-Catholic in religion, a classist in literature and a royalist in politics." This kind of self-analysis might be as accurate as any more complex statement (Kaplan, 1997:5).

Modern poetry, like history, records everything, which belongs to tradition and religion. Kaplan believes that, "Modern literature and particularly modern poetry is the heir of many schools and traditions" (Kaplan, 1997:9). It was not sprung only out of the modern age. He sees that modern poetry is the combination of both metaphysical poetry, which was introduced by John Donne (1571[?]-1631) and the symbolist poetry, which was introduced by Etienne Stéphan (1842-1898). The symbolists helped hastening the disintegration of the modern world by a derangement of the senses so that by recombining the exploded elements with little or no relations to their former structures, they might construct a truer inner reality (Kaplan, 1997: 9-10). Kaplan also points out:

> Since grammar, syntax, and structure are also logical entities
> related to semantics, the symbolists discarded or even
> exaggerated traditional usage. The metaphysical poets, on the
> other hand, used their entire intellectual as well as their intuitive
> and suggestive resources to bring congruity to discordant ideas
> and images (Kaplan, 1997: 9).

Eliot was under the influence of many literary figures and schools, like, the French symbolists, especially Arthur Symons. Through reading Symons' book, *The Symbolist Movement in Poetry*, Eliot was acquainted with Jack Laforgue's poetry. In many of his poems, written between 1909 and 1911, culminating in *Portrait of a Lady* and *The Love Song of J. Alfred, Prufrock*, Eliot adapted and developed such aspects of Laforgue's style as his different juxtapositions of imagery and of diction. (McGowan, 2004: 63). Eliot was also under the influence of Ezra Pound, by whose help his poems were published (Kermode, 2003: Ix-Ivx).

Many writers wrote about the problems of modern man, but none of them made it the focus of their works as Eliot did. Modern man's image, his likings and dislikings, conduct, and beliefs are prominently depicted in his poetry: Man suffers excessively in terms of emotional vitality. Modern man lives according to the social conventions and the rules of a decadent culture. Man's life is partly sordid and sensual. He is to an extent aware of his isolation and alienation. He feels himself entangled in a corrupt, decaying, ugly society. All the features of the modern man could be categorized into three major groups. Each group, in turn, would show a series of relating problems, which would make a whole entity. The duplicity of man, lack of communication and man's isolation are three basic unpleasant situations of the modern life, making him more and more alienated. The sense of duplicity was very common within modern man, which Eliot showed in his poetry. Indeed, the speaker of modernist poems wrestles with the fundamental question of the "self," often feeling fragmented and alienated from the world around him. In other words, a coherent speaker with a clear sense of himself / herself is hard to be found in modernist poetry, often leaving readers confused and "lost." The issue of modernism is crucial in one's understanding of Eliot's poetry, especially in *The Love Song of J. Alfred Prufrock* since it is "now recognized as the first full-fledged modernist poem" where "Eliot may be said to have invented modernism" (Lauter, 2005:299).

Nidhi Tiwari and Jaydipsinh Dodiya in their book, *Critical Perspectives on T.S. Eliot's Poetry*, concluded that T. S. Eliot has created natural scenes, and dealt with natural tendency in his poetry. In order to satisfy his sentiments, he tries to represent temporal tendency to mould things mirroring the reality of the image in the mind, which is not easy to be debated completely, except by Eliot. A powerful undercurrent of reality always marks T. S. Eliot's poetry, and offer the quality of intellectuality to his poetry. A reader's response is mostly subject to its appeal to the mind. When reading his poetry, readers immediately confront intellectual hazards of image, symbol, thought, belief, and notions. Eliot uses a philosophical method to probe the truth; (Tiwari and Jaydipsinh, 2005: 6).

T. S. Eliot was an introspective man who had been even a shy and solitary boy. He achieved worldwide fame in his early thirties. The Publication of *The Waste Land* in 1922 established him as a benchmark figure against whom other writers would thereafter be measured. He had been reasonably famous in the English-speaking world even before 1922; in England, in particular, he had been known as a poet, critic and journalist. Whatever poetry Eliot wrote after *The Waste Land* was imitated, attacked and defended. He won the Noble Prize for literature in 1948 because he was one of the great innovative poets of the twentieth century. Eliot was probably probing basic and deeply sensitive veins of twentieth century existence just as surely as, albeit in different ways from, Freud and Marx. William Butler Yeats, Wallace Stevens and other major twentieth-century poets do not have the same sort of social focus. Yeats' passion is personal and he himself is the centre of his poetry and thought, and Stevens is also a passionate man but it tends towards the passion of the mind (Raffel, 1982: 2-3).

It is said that the works of Joseph Conrad especially *Heart of Darkness*, had a great influence on T. S. Eliot, but he rearranges and presents everything, in such innovative new way that leaves his own mark on whatever he uses:

> Eliot has so clearly and firmly created and sustained his own
> style that it is his quality which we feel when we encounter
> some of the sources from which it derives. Because Eliot has

repeated the accents of Laforgue and Conrad for his own controlled purposes, we discover that he has left something of his own accent on their language—he has turned our ears to hear them in a special way (Unger, 1961:21).

As a young man, Eliot adopted from Charles Maurras and the long tradition of French reactionary thought an advocacy of "classicism." This term, in France, covered the whole range of antagonisms against the revolution of 1789. It aligned readers against romanticism, democracy, and Protestantism. This opposition was organized on behalf of the Latin tradition in literature, as well as royalism, Catholicism, and a rigidly hierarchical social organization culminating in hereditary aristocracy. In Maurras's version, this was coloured by hostility towards the Jew. Maurras articulated this position eloquently and ushered it into the new century in a copious outpouring of books, articles, and pamphlets on a range of topics: literary criticism, political theory, religion, economics, and comparative culture. It can be observed that Maurrasien inheritance provided Eliot with a dominant intellectual framework that he retained throughout his life. This is not to say that no change occurred over a career, that spanned half a century; after Maurras's condemnation by the Vatican in 1926, Eliot worked feverishly to realign the component parts of this ideology, subordinating everything to religion, as he wrote to Paul Elmer More in 1936, "I am very happy you like the essay on religion and literature." What is constant is that the political dimension that was the focal point of the Maurrasien compound was advanced in sub rosa almost usually in Eliot. Early in his career, Eliot presented classicism to an English audience as nearly exclusively a literary preference, something easy enough to be given general ignorance of the term's full implication in France. His unwillingness to be more open was due in a large part to the fact that he was a more scrupulous thinker than Maurras himself in general and he was unsure exactly how the politics, religion, and literature necessarily entailed one another. This difficulty was exacerbated by the fact that he was trying to impose classicism on a traditionally Protestant country (a problem registered in his later reference to Anglicanism as Anglo-Catholicism). Immediately upon the Vatican's condemnation of Maurras for valuing Catholicism primarily for its political function, Eliot began taking religious instruction in the Anglican faith and was accepted into the communion the following year. Thereafter, though opposing the same antagonists, he engaged them in the name of the Christian commonwealth. Politics led Eliot to religion but he rarely acknowledged the political element that constituted a central part of what he understood (Asher, 1998: 8-9).

By the use of various images throughout his poetry, Eliot could portray the cares and wishes of modern man. Imagism was a movement that appeared between 1909 and 1917. It flourished in Britain and in the United States for a brief period. Imagism had three principles," as articulated by Pound: the direct treatment of the 'thing,' whether subjective or objective; the rejection of any words that do not contribute to the presentation of the image; and composition in the sequence of a musical phrase not in a sequence of a metronome" (T. E. Hulme, 1955: 74). As part of the modernist movement, away from the sentimentality and moralizing tone of the nineteenth-century Victorian poetry, imagist poets used a new technique to help them create a new poetic expression. The imagists studied and were influenced by the French symbolists, who were experimenting with free verse (*vers libre*); a verse form that used a cadence that mimicked natural speech rather than the accustomed rhythm of metrical feet, or lines. Rules of rhyming were also considered nonessential. Pound, however, was the primary theorist. The main principle involved, modeled in part on the Japanese haiku, was that the image was not to be "described" but created with precision and brevity (Miller, 2005:270). In *A Few Don'ts* by an Imagiste published in *Poetry* in March 1913, Pound defined the Image as "that which presents an intellectual and emotional complex in an instant of time" (Miller, Ibid).

The early beginning of the twentieth century Poets in all countries, employed imagism to enhance their expression and create a greater impact on the reader. Kristian Smidit has defined poetry in this way:

> Poetry is the language of actual thought, or actual ideas. Its actuality is not merely contingent and does not merely lie in its faithfulness to an external subject matter: it resides far more in its faithfulness to the movements of the mind and the spirit of the poet, which manifested in the poetic use of imagery. For actual thought, also tends to move in images (Smidit, 1961: 110).

This definition indicates that imagery is inseparable from poetry. The image that is used here is a mental picture. Imagists decided to give up the Romantic mode of expression. An Imagist anthology was published in 1914 that collected works by William Carlos Williams, Richard Aldington, and James Joyce, as well as Hilda Doolittle and Pound. By the time the anthology appeared, Amy Lowell had effectively appropriated Imagism and was seen as the movement's leader. Three years later, even Amy Lowell thought the movement had run its course. Pound by then was claiming that he invented Imagism to launch H.D.'s career. Though Imagism as a movement was over by 1917, the ideas about poetry embedded in the Imagist doctrine profoundly influenced free verse poets throughout the twentieth century. Imagism was a reaction against the flabby abstract language and "careless thinking" of Georgian Romanticism. Imagist poetry aimed to replace muddy abstractions with exactness of observed detail, apt metaphors, and economy of language. For example, Pound's *In a Station of the Metro* started from a glimpse of beautiful faces in a dark subway and elevated that perception into a crisp vision by finding an intensified equivalent image. The metaphor provokes a sharp, intuitive discovery in order to get at the essence of life. The movement sprang from ideas developed by T.E. Hulme, who as early as 1908 was proposing to the Poets' Club in London poetry based on absolutely accurate presentation of its subject with no excess of meaningless words. The first tenet of the Imagist manifesto was "To use the language of common speech, but to employ always the exact word, not the nearly-exact, nor the merely decorative word." Images made poetry to be understood by the readers clearly; but for Eliot, the use of images and symbols made his poetry obscure and difficult. Hugh Kenner called Eliot *The invisible poet*, but the quality of using images made his poetry attractive. Changes that took place in the twentieth century affected both form and content of poetry; in terms of form the French symbolist poets offered Eliot "urban life" and "vers libre", (Thorne, 2006: 287). The poet turns away from decadent Romantic tradition. Eliot sees life in realism and the most commonplace subjects are considered suitable for the modern life. In his essay *"Tradition and the Individual Talent"*, Eliot states that it is not the duty of the poet to create a beautiful world. The poet should try to see beneath both beauty and ugliness to see the horror, boredom and glory (Tiwari, 2001:1-4).

It is possible to divide Eliot's poetry into three phases. The first, period includes those poems, which express the disillusionment of the post World War I, the second covers the period of his conversion to Anglicanism in 1927, in which he struggles with the intellectual difficulties of the religious faith, and the final period is a period with a large gap in his writing of nearly 15 years. This period ends with the "Four Quartets". The modern readers might say, "This is Eliot's solution to the problems of modern life, but I can be neither a classist nor a royalist nor a converter to Anglo-Catholicism. For such a reader the early works will almost certainly be more rewarding" (Walsh, 2007:175).

In his book, *The Durable Satisfactions of Life*, Charles, Eliot William says that the modern man in the twentieth century has hardly had any appreciation for religion, especially for Christianity. The modern mind craves an immediate motif and leads well for today. The new religion builds on the actual experiences of men, women and of human society as a whole (Eliot, 1910: 197).

It is said that the past is always an essential part of the present. The psychological weaknesses and experiences of ancients are substantially similar to those of the modern's. Eliot believed that modern man should return to the classical masters like, Homer and Dante (Cuddy, 2000: 21). Thorne comments that Eliot's interest in the works of the French Symbolists was because of their belief that it was impossible to use the conventional language to express feelings as the nineteenth century poets actually faced such kind of a problem. Eliot believed that the poet should create a special language of symbols that suggests the vague nature of experience to the reader in which a direct statement or description cannot represent real experience, but they believed that only a succession of images could convey the true meaning of consciousness. Imagists who are very direct and objective and they focused on the concrete rather than the abstract. Eliot tries to convey the essence of life rather than escaping from grinding nature of reality. Eliot's images function in a different way, which often take on a symbolic significance (Thorne, 2006: 279-280).

Eliot, who was trained in classics, was described as a man of keen intellect, capable of developing a philosophical aspect in his poetry, which is a new way of writing poetry. It has also been confirmed that he was better equipped than any other poet to bring verse fully into the twentieth century. James Joyce remarked of Eliot in a notebook that he abolished the idea of poetry for ladies; by this he gave modern poetry one of its most distinctive features (Ellmann and O'Clair, 1988: 479). Many critics and scholars refer to Eliot's philosophical training when reading his poetry. The symbols, which Eliot used are not easy for the readers to understand therefore, they connect his poetry with philosophy. There is no doubt that there are ways in which his interests in ideas have influenced his poetry. Deutch and Flam believe that some study of the primitive life is needed in order to understand modern man; so "some study of primitive man furthers our understanding of civilized man" (Deutch and Flam, 2003: 122) The wide variety of interpretations of how those ideas are actually presented in his poetry suggests that perhaps poetry was not the preferred medium for the elaboration of his thinking. One could declare that philosophy is far more important to his prose, both his critical works and his cultural criticism. Poetry, for Eliot, was the means through which he worked out the practical consequences of action and faith (Cooper, 2006: 28).

Modern man has been described as a person who voyages in the sea of life, and never stops. The journey differs from one person to another but there is no doubt about his being a seeker of his rights and perhaps true identity in his society. This does not mean that everyone can succeed in reaching his destination, because social or fatal obstacles are in front of him (Tiwari, 2001: 21).

The process of transition of human life from one stage to another means giving up the old life and starting a new one, often leading to a feeling of alienation, estrangement from the previous state. These transitions naturally differ from one individual to another, depending on the surrounding circumstances and personal understanding of what is happening. As an expatriate, his psychological, social and religious concerns made these developments in Eliot's poetry inevitable. E. M. Forster wrote of Eliot's religion, "what he seeks is not revelation but stability." The quest for psychological stability is central in Eliot's works. The social and personal agony of *The Waste Land* and the individual agony of Prufrock are responses to the instability of the modern world (Schmidt, 1979: 125-126).

Eliot's poetry holds the mirror up to the modern urban complex culture. It portrays the post-industrial image of modern man; therefore, to understand Eliot means understanding the spirit of modernism

(Sarker.2008: 1). The great influence of Eliot on the poetry of the twentieth century according to Sheila Sullivan "for good or ill . . . has been immeasurable". After the publication of *The Love Song of J. Alfred Prufrock* in 1917 and *The Waste Land* in 1922, it was no longer possible for any poet to write in the manner of the Georgians. His poetry emerged exactly matching the manner to the intention, and from the beginning, his touch was lethal to the Georgian style. With Pound and Laforgue behind him, Eliot created a revolution in modern poetry (Sullivan, 1973: III).

Eliot believed that the role of the poet was to bring order to the irregular, fragmentary experience of life, transmuting ideas into sensations and amalgamating disparate experience. This belief was to make his poems into a sequence of cinematic images, which represent his own view of the world. He also believed that poets should find ways to express implicitly without using romantic outpouring of feelings or sentimentality. Thorne says Eliot believed that the only way of expressing emotion in the form of art, is by finding an "objective correlative", i.e., a set of objects, a situation and a chain of events which shall be the formula of that particular emotion; that means, when the external facts, which must terminate sensory experience, are given, the emotion is immediately evoked (Thorne, 2006: 282).

Eliot's response to the tormenting complexity of his age, which was continually modified and renewed as he suffered and matured, is a response to the immense panorama of futility and anarchy which contemporary history was essentially moral and spiritual. His principal purpose in life as a poet and man of letters was to find a way of controlling and ordering, of giving shape and significance to the chaotic fragmentation and alienation of the life of modern man. He thought that the overriding problem of modern man i.e., alienation which was the result of anarchic individualism and scientific regimentation, could be solved merely at the religious level of man's spiritual existence. Because the requisite outlook can grow only out of religion, which comprehends the entire aspects of life and effectively counteracts the futility and anarchy of contemporary social life, Eliot believed that only in the realms of religion and art the problems of the modern society can be solved (Singh, 2001: 267). There are different viewpoints among the critics of Eliot's poetry, for instance Mishra, in his book, *The Poetry of T. S. Eliot*, states that Dutta Roy's thesis, which studies the meaning of Eliot's poetry, mistakenly says that in art and poetry God is at the centre of Eliot's poetry. He is against this and states that Eliot has placed man at the centre of his poetry (Mishra, 2003: 18).

It is said that curiosity and wariness about language and culture emerge very early in Eliot's intellectual life. It is seen in the comments and observations he wrote during his university years and in his doctoral thesis, *Knowledge and Experience in the Philosophy of F. H. Bradley* (1916). But this focus on language took its most important form, not from his philosophical studies intrinsically, but in his poetry and in his criticism. The causes of this turn to language in the twentieth century are many and complex but perhaps the most important reason for a poet, the one that captures the mood of Eliot's early and even some of his late poetry, has been described best by the German philosopher Heidegger in his comments about the despoiling of language as a vital medium for connection in modern times. He argues that in modernity,

> Language in general is worn out and used up as an indispensable but master less means of communication that may be used as one pleases, as indifferent as a means of public transport, as a street car which everyone rides in. Everyone speaks and writes away in the language, without hindrance and above all without danger (Heidegger, 1961: 42)

Cooper says that Heidegger continues to say that only "a very few" of the poets are cable of bringing language back to life from the death-in-life into which it has fallen in modern times. This is the special task of poets and Eliot seems to have understood this as his own particular poetic task. The possibilities of making poetry from a fallen language, a language exhausted by use, "worn down by the non-stop tracing pedestrian chatter and triteness, was suggested by his reading of the poetry of Charles Baudelaire and Jules Laforgue" (Cooper, 2006: 41).

Societies in their organization and historical development are predetermined by economic or technological considerations (Kaplan, 2006: 5).

The most controversial aspect of the modern movement was its rejection of tradition. Modernism's stress on freedom of expression, experimentation, radicalism, and primitivism disregards conventional expectations. In many forms of art, that controversy over the rejection of tradition often meant startling and alienating audiences with bizarre and unpredictable effects, the strange and disturbing combinations of motifs in Surrealism, and the use of extreme dissonance and atonality in modernist music. The technique of modern literature is often involved in the rejection of intelligible plots or characterization in novels, or the invention in poetry that rejected clear interpretation. The Soviet Communist government rejected modernism after the rise of Stalin on the grounds of alleged elitism, although it had previously gave approval to Futurism and Constructivism, and the Nazi government in Germany considered it narcissistic and ridiculous (Berghaus, 2000: 212). The Nazis exhibited modernist paintings alongside with works which were considered the mentally ill in an exhibition entitled *Degenerate Art*. In fact, modernism flourished mainly in consumer/capitalist societies, despite the fact that its proponents often rejected consumerism itself. However, high modernism began to merge with consumer culture after World War II, especially during the 1960s. The likes of Bob Dylan, Serge Gainsbourg and *The Rolling Stones* combined popular musical traditions with modernist verse, adopting literary devices derived from James Joyce, Samuel Beckett, James Thurber, T. S. Eliot, Guillaume Apollinaire, Allen Ginsberg, and others. Modernist design also began to enter the mainstream of popular culture, as simplified and stylized forms, which were often associated with dreams of a space age high-tech future that became popular. This merging of consumer and high versions of modernist culture resulted in a radical transformation of the meaning of "modernism" (Grant, 1999: 100). Firstly, it implied that a movement based on the rejection of tradition had become a tradition of its own, and secondly, it demonstrated that the distinction between elite modernist and mass consumerist culture had lost its quality of being precise. Some writers declared that modernism had become institutionalized, and in some other fields, the effects of modernism have remained the strongest.

Modern poetry is known as being very unusual, and obscure. The heart of this vagueness mirrors the complexity of the modern life and its problems because poetry has been a medium for reflecting the entire problems of modern man. The problems are artistically reflected in the poetry of T.S. Eliot. Eliot's poetry is similar to the metaphysical poetry because he, like the metaphysical poets, uses conventional images in a startling way and creates new images by using unexpected literary devices like, metaphor, and juxtaposition and linked very far-fetched ideas in his poetry. For instance, in *The Love of Song of J. Alfred Prufrock*, the opening simile of "the patient etherized upon a table" sets the tone for the images, which follow in the poem (Thorne, 2006:289).

Modern poetry dramatizes the problems of the modern age, which permeates experience in terms of values, ethics, social and psychological problems. Modern poets are different from the romantic poets, who tried to find solutions for individual's problems. However, modern poets seek to understand this split of modern man in a modern way. The sense of incompleteness, alienation and that of irrecoverable loss of existence without spiritual centre has nowhere been cleverly dramatized than in *The Hollow Men* (Shakti, Batra, 2001: 3-5).

English and American modern poetry had several independent voices that question contemporary important events and catastrophes of the age. The most important aspect of modern poetry is the special way of perceiving life and dealing with the world, because of the radical changes brought about by the first and second world wars. The destructive results of these two wars led to the creation of a new type of poetry, which was quite different from the poetry before the war in content and style, i.e., the poetry of the Victorian age at the late nineteenth century and the early beginning of the twentieth century. The devastating results of World War I caused a change in many European countries and brought about radical changes in the social life and disillusionment among people. The great losses faced by a large number of people in different countries changed the way people perceived religion, tradition and ethics, which created a shake in their beliefs and even in their political ideologies. Theologians, public intellectuals, and academicians argued that the forces of modernization were so powerful that they inevitably secularized western society and rendered religious belief old-fashioned. Churches and religious movements were doomed to extinction. But Balmar in his book, *Religion in Twentieth Century America,* states, nothing could be far from the truth. "Instead of dying, religion has thrived as never before. Whether measured by church attendance rates, national opinion polls, or charitable activities, this nation, arguably the most modern in the world, is also the most religious." (Balmar, 2001: 7)

The poetry of the age mirrors the new social, religious and political changes in the life of the people and their disillusionment. World War I was a very sad and catastrophic experience for the entire European countries and of the world in general, but its impact was much greater on the intellectual people. (Batra, 2001: 3-5). It was after that destructive war that some modern poets like Eliot brought a new way of writing poetry "In defining themselves as innovative, Eliot and Pound rejected much Victorian literature for its out-moded Romanticism" (Cronin etal, 2002: 513).

Tiwari states that Cleanth Brook points out that Eliot, like John Donne, belonged to the tradition of wit and paradox in English poetry. In his poetry, Eliot has portrayed the atmosphere of crime and the horror faced by humanity in the modern societies. Eliot has used the Greek myth in his poetry because he, like the symbolists, found a very deep spirituality in Greek mythology, which was quite different from the vulgarity of the modern world surrounding them. Eliot and the symbolist poets tried to present a picture of the ideal life in contrast to the debasement of values of the world in which modern man lives (Tiwari, 2001:1-3).

It is clear that Eliot knew when and why he decided to become a poet. He became a poet at the age of fourteen in 1902, after he read a copy of Fitz Gerard's free translation of *The Rubáiyát of Omar Khayyam*, which had left an impact on his imagination (Jr. Miller, 2005:2). In the winter of 1910-1911, when Eliot was studying in Paris, he read three of Dostoevsky's novels *Crime and Punishment, The idiot* and *The Brothers Karamazov*, on which he comments that "These three novels made a very profound impression on me and I had read them all before Prufrock was completed" (Southam, 1968: 18).

The poetry of Eliot, on the one hand, shows the catastrophes faced by modern man, like alienation, and on the other hand, suggests the solution for each single problem. Lewis Feuer argues that the problem of modern man is not specifically modern, it is omnipresent. "What stands out from a historical and comparative standpoint is the omnipresence of alienation; it takes different guises in all societies" (Feuer, 1969, 90).

It is said that the lack of basic wisdom is one of the salient characteristics of Eliot's poetry. Eliot's poetic revolution was complex in its effects. In fact, he introduced the urban element into his work as an essential and vital change in poetry; but Eliot's imitators gave the readers the notion that his poetry is obscure without the essential vision and wisdom that underlie the originality and made a virtue out of incomprehensibility (Stephen Martin, 1984: 97).

Marlowe. A. Miller in his book, *Masterpieces of British Modernism* states that Virginia Woolf has declared that human nature, and human relations changed at about 1910. This change included master-slave relationship and that of the family members; especially between the parents and their children (Miller, 2006: 1). Any change in the human nature results in changes in viewing religion, conduct and most of the aspects of life. Woolf's comment refers to those radical changes in those aspects of the modern society, which paved the way for the new poetry in many countries like America and the United Kingdom.

T.S. Eliot has been accused of "obscurity and pretentiousness" (Southam, 1974:15). Eliot touched the question of difficulty in modern poetry. He said that difficulty is not something peculiar to certain writers but a condition of writing in the contemporary world. In a context of "great variety and complexity", the modern poet can only respond with "various and complex results": "The poet must become more and more comprehensive, more allusive, more indirect to force, to dislocate if necessary, language into his meaning." Much of Eliot's poetry can be read with pleasure at the first sight, although it might not be fully grasped; Eliot points out in this regard saying: "I know that some of the poetry to which I am most devoted is poetry to which I did not understand at first reading", and also insists that when poetry calls for knowledge, the poetry-lover must be prepared to answer the demand (Southam, 1974:16).

A factor that obstructed the development of American poetry was the vast distance among the poets who showed some talent, and may have thrived in a center, which did not allow them communicate with one another. On the contrary, London was that center where the writers could meet and communicate, but the United States saw no movement at the end of the century like the 1890s poets in London who rebelled against the Victorian moralities and the late nineteenth-century version of Romanticism. Outside the Harvard and

New York centers, American poets worked alone to educate themselves by benefiting from the anthologies of English poetry. Frustration with the cultural climate of the United States had already, by the turn of the century, led to the mass exodus to Europe, of the painters, like Whistler(1834-1903) and Mary Cassatt (1844-1926), and the writers like Henry James (1843-1916), Gertrude Stein (1874-1946), then Pound (1885-1972), Hilda Doolittle (1886-1961), and T. S. Eliot (1888-1965), and later in 1920s to a generation of expatriates, including Ernest Hemingway (1899-1961) and F. Scott Fitzgerald (1896-1940), (MacGowan, 2004: 11).

1910 was the year King Edward VII died and the year that woman's demands to obtain the vote (suffrage) gained momentum and met violent police retaliation.1910 was also the final year of the dominance of the Liberal Party over England. Whether one accepts the date (1910) suggested by Woolf or not, it is obvious that modernists occupied the first forty years of the twentieth century. (Miller, 2006:1). Virginia Woolf links the changes, which occurred in the twentieth century, to the radical shift in the modern world caused by World War I. In "How It Strikes a Contemporary" written in 1923, Woolf states "we are sharply cut off from our predecessors. A shift in the scale—the war, the sudden slip of masses held in position for ages—has shaken the fabric from top to bottom, alienated us from the past" (The Essays, Vol. 4, 238). For speaking of the aims of the modern poets, Henderson and Monroe quoted Mr. Yeats's speech, who states that,

> We were weary of the art of Tennyson and his imitators. We wanted to get rid not only of rhetoric but also of poetic diction. We tried to strip away everything that was artificial, to get a style like speech, as simple as the simplest prose, like a cry of the heart (Henderson and Monroe, 1917: I X).

This was a much more serious challenge for the modern poets against the Victorians (Kreizenbec, 2004: 29). Eliot, who was against the romantic poets, wrote, "the decay of these poets mostly depends on their too much self. For a great artist, an awareness of the world outside of himself is necessary, his personal of the consciousness of the general humanity." Eliot supports the Aristotelian notion that poetry is the philosophy of writing. Its object is truth, not individual or local but general operative. In the writing of a serious poem, the poet has to be too responsible in revealing the truth; which must not be harmed by fantasies (Rao, 1996: 21). "Eliot's history is static, though tradition shows modifications" Rampal points out that Eliot in his essay *Tradition and the Individual Talent*, declares that poets are required to be aware of the whole literature of Europe since it mirrors the history and the traditions of Europe and via their awareness they can enrich their poetry (Rampal, 1996: 88). Eliot believes that a writer must develop consciousness of the past and he should try hard to develop his consciousness throughout his career. Eliot believes that the modern poets have enhanced their writings on the tradition, and it needs not to be accepted by the society (Rampal, 1996: 77). What makes Eliot one of the most famous modern writers is his derivation of his concept of time from diverse sources, which he had shaped into the theory of history and tradition.

The poet must not be only inspired but also calculative, thoughtful and responsible. Eliot further argues that,

> It is essential to establish a vital connection between the individual and the race. The struggle in art is to make the poet aware of the mind of the Europe. A mind which leaves in time is considered to be more important than his own private mind (Eliot's Sacred Wood).

The very early years of the twentieth century witnessed the rebirth and transformation of poetry. Like the novelists, the poets wished to renew their art and tried to keep a distance from the stagnant condition of late Victorian literature. One of the pioneers of the modern poetry is W.B.Yeats (1865-1939) who strived to leave the conventions of the Victorian period and in the second decade of the twentieth century, Yeats was able to move away from the Celtic myths and legends that dominated his early works and used the contemporary political and social issues directly in his poetry. Gilles and Mahood state that,

> the vibrancy of the poetry in this period is remarkable, with a wide range of poetic movements emerging; each contested the others' aesthetics, through the various manifestos that they produced and published little magazines, many of which were founded and run by the poets themselves (Gillies and Mahood, 2007: 64-65).

There are some misunderstandings among the critics concerning Eliot's poetry. In 1931, Eliot stated that when he wrote *The Waste Land* some of the critics said that he had expressed the "disillusionment of a generation", which "is nonsense". Eliot commented that he may express modern man's illusion of being disillusioned, but this was not part of Eliot's intension (Sandra, 1999: 530-531). Part of what is said concerning Eliot's poetry is not deniable because he is a very sensitive poet who has written about his own psychological problems and since he lived in the same society he may have similar problems with the other people because of the two destructive World Wars, which destroyed modern society. But the other part of what the critics said concerning Eliot's poetry is not believable because Eliot himself denied that and declared that he wrote his poems for himself. It can be said that Eliot's problems are like the problems of modern man, in this sense via Eliot's problems one can recognize the problems of the modern man; furthermore, Eliot is the representative of modern man that can express his sense of alienation, failure of communication as well as lack of confidence.

Ezra Pound is one of those who had left a very great influence on Eliot; when he, for the first time, showed Pound his poem *The Love Song of J. Alfred Prufrock,* he declared "he had found an American poet who had actually trained himself and modernized himself on his own" (Sandra, 1999:532). Pound's statement indicates that Eliot was not an ordinary poet. It also indicates that Eliot has enhanced his own poetry by depending on his efforts wherever he was. When a person leaves his country and joins another country his life becomes complicated and he may even give up his writing though life for Eliot became very difficult but he did not give up writing poetry but also made the quality of his work better if compared to his previous works.

Eliot's death, on January 4, 1965, at the age of seventy-six, marked the end of a bright period in English literary history. Twentieth century is the period when Eliot was the pathfinder for the other poets during his time (Batra, 2001:1). The appeal of his genius was not limited only to the English-speaking people or to the European tradition. Thus, one can say that Eliot is English, a European and a universal poet because of his influence on world literature of the twentieth century, and has been one of the great dominant forces in English literature of the twentieth century. If any reader wants to understand Eliot's poetry, he should read the whole body of his writing, not only his poetic and dramatic productions but also his religious and cultural criticism as well as his editorial works at the British publishing house (Faber and Faber). One can see his role in the modern world in general and in modern poetry in particular (Damrosch and Dettmar, 2006: 2506).

In his book *T.S. Eliot's Major Poems and Plays*, Kaplan says:

> No single poet has influenced the development of modern American poetry quite as much as T.S. Eliot, both as poet and critic. His serious publication appeared in 1915; Henry James (1843-1916) was still alive; indeed, Emerson and Longfellow had died only some thirty years earlier, and Whitman, Wittier and Holmes only some twenty years earlier. Eliot is roughly contemporary with the generation of Edwin Arlington Robinson, Robert Frost, Carl Standburg, Vachel Lindsay, Willa Cather, H. L. Mencken, Sinclair Lewis, and Robison Jeffers (Kaplan, 1997: 5).

This shows that Eliot was one of the earliest modern poets. His coming in the beginning of the twentieth century is startling, for Eliot's poetry was as different from the poetry of the nineteenth century as it was different from that of the fifteenth century. There are many literary figures by which Eliot was influenced like, Byron, Bergson, Babbitt, as well as the French symbolists. Eliot combined these influences with the pessimistic view of modern man and used them in his poetry and the critical works, which have largely shaped the English and American modern poetry. Dwivedi confirms the same argument, and points out that the role of the American poets of the twentieth century cannot be neglected. In his book entitled *T. S. Eliot, The Critical Study*, Dwivedi points out that Eliot was not only a poet but also a critic and a playwright and highlights that "Eliot's images are drawn directly from life or his own experiences and knowledge. They are an integral part of his eventful life." (Dwivedi, 2002: 35).

Eliot's role as a literary figure was prominent, and his influence is obviously seen in many fields like poetry, drama and literary criticism, religious and social thought. "However, his importance as a critic and as a religious and social thinker was and still is felt in so diffused and oblique a manner that it seemed fitting to confine the area of interest to his poetry and plays" (Grant, 1982: 1). Yeats' comment on T.S. Eliot, in his introduction to *The Oxford Book of Modern Verse* suggests an intimate understanding of the ethos of a religious person. He says: "Eliot's religion compared to that of John Gray, Francis Thomson, Lionel Johnson in *The Dark Angel* lacks all strong emotion; a New England Protestant by decent, there is little self-surrender in his personal relation to God and the soul" (Yeats. W.B, OBMV1975: XXII).

The sense of failure, which Eliot has expressed in a psychological symbolism, is derived from Freud, and to some degree from Jung. Eliot mixes the technique of "free verse" with the colloquial conversation which echoes his sense of kinship with the juxtapositions of the past and the present time, to reflect both his philosophical concern with the modern time, and his belief in the past as important in terms of meaningful ritual and tradition.

It is probably this latter conviction, which led him to give up "young" America for the older civilization of England and the old rituals of the Church of England. In his introduction to *For Lancelot Andrews*, Eliot describes himself as "an Anglo-Catholic in religion, a classist in literature and a royalist in politics." This kind of self-analysis might be as accurate as any more complex statement (Kaplan, 1997:5).

Modern poetry, like history, records everything, which belongs to tradition and religion. Kaplan believes that, "Modern literature and particularly modern poetry is the heir of many schools and traditions" (Kaplan, 1997:9). It was not sprung only out of the modern age. He sees that modern poetry is the combination of both metaphysical poetry, which was introduced by John Donne (1571[?]-1631) and the symbolist poetry, which was introduced by Etienne Stéphan (1842-1898). The symbolists helped hastening the disintegration of the modern world by a derangement of the senses so that by recombining the exploded elements with little or no relations to their former structures, they might construct a truer inner reality (Kaplan, 1997: 9-10). Kaplan also points out:

> Since grammar, syntax, and structure are also logical entities related to semantics, the symbolists discarded or even exaggerated traditional usage. The metaphysical poets, on the other hand, used their entire intellectual as well as their intuitive and suggestive resources to bring congruity to discordant ideas and images (Kaplan, 1997: 9).

Eliot was under the influence of many literary figures and schools, like, the French symbolists, especially Arthur Symons. Through reading Symons' book, *The Symbolist Movement in Poetry*, Eliot was acquainted with Jack Laforgue's poetry. In many of his poems, written between 1909 and 1911, culminating in *Portrait of a Lady* and *The Love Song of J. Alfred, Prufrock*, Eliot adapted and developed such aspects of Laforgue's style as his different juxtapositions of imagery and of diction. (McGowan, 2004: 63). Eliot was also under the influence of Ezra Pound, by whose help his poems were published (Kermode, 2003: Ix-Ivx).

Many writers wrote about the problems of modern man, but none of them made it the focus of their works as Eliot did. Modern man's image, his likings and dislikings, conduct, and beliefs are prominently depicted in his poetry: Man suffers excessively in terms of emotional vitality. Modern man lives according to the social conventions and the rules of a decadent culture. Man's life is partly sordid and sensual. He is to an extent aware of his isolation and alienation. He feels himself entangled in a corrupt, decaying, ugly society. All the features of the modern man could be categorized into three major groups. Each group, in turn, would show a series of relating problems, which would make a whole entity. The duplicity of man, lack of communication and man's isolation are three basic unpleasant situations of the modern life, making him more and more alienated. The sense of duplicity was very common within modern man, which Eliot showed in his poetry. Indeed, the speaker of modernist poems wrestles with the fundamental question of the "self," often feeling fragmented and alienated from the world around him. In other words, a coherent speaker with a clear sense of himself / herself is hard to be found in modernist poetry, often leaving readers confused and "lost." The issue of modernism is crucial in one's understanding of Eliot's poetry, especially in *The Love Song of J. Alfred Prufrock* since it is "now recognized as the first full-fledged modernist poem" where "Eliot may be said to have invented modernism" (Lauter, 2005:299).

Nidhi Tiwari and Jaydipsinh Dodiya in their book, *Critical Perspectives on T.S. Eliot's Poetry*, concluded that T. S. Eliot has created natural scenes, and dealt with natural tendency in his poetry. In order to satisfy his sentiments, he tries to represent temporal tendency to mould things mirroring the reality of the image in the mind, which is not easy to be debated completely, except by Eliot. A powerful undercurrent of reality always marks T. S. Eliot's poetry, and offer the quality of intellectuality to his poetry. A reader's response is mostly subject to its appeal to the mind. When reading his poetry, readers immediately confront intellectual hazards of image, symbol, thought, belief, and notions. Eliot uses a philosophical method to probe the truth; (Tiwari and Jaydipsinh, 2005: 6).

T. S. Eliot was an introspective man who had been even a shy and solitary boy. He achieved worldwide fame in his early thirties. The Publication of *The Waste Land* in 1922 established him as a benchmark figure against whom other writers would thereafter be measured. He had been reasonably famous in the English-speaking world even before 1922; in England, in particular, he had been known as a poet, critic and journalist. Whatever poetry Eliot wrote after *The Waste Land* was imitated, attacked and defended. He won the Noble Prize for literature in 1948 because he was one of the great innovative poets of the twentieth century. Eliot was probably probing basic and deeply sensitive veins of twentieth century existence just as surely as, albeit in different ways from, Freud and Marx. William Butler Yeats, Wallace Stevens and other major twentieth-century poets do not have the same sort of social focus. Yeats' passion is personal and he himself is the centre of his poetry and thought, and Stevens is also a passionate man but it tends towards the passion of the mind (Raffel, 1982: 2-3).

It is said that the works of Joseph Conrad especially *Heart of Darkness*, had a great influence on T. S. Eliot, but he rearranges and presents everything, in such innovative new way that leaves his own mark on whatever he uses:

> Eliot has so clearly and firmly created and sustained his own style that it is his quality which we feel when we encounter some of the sources from which it derives. Because Eliot has repeated the accents of Laforgue and Conrad for his own controlled purposes, we discover that he has left something of his own accent on their language—he has turned our ears to hear them in a special way (Unger, 1961:21).

As a young man, Eliot adopted from Charles Maurras and the long tradition of French reactionary thought an advocacy of "classicism."

This term, in France, covered the whole range of antagonisms against the revolution of 1789. It aligned readers against romanticism, democracy, and Protestantism. This opposition was organized on behalf of the Latin tradition in literature, as well as royalism, Catholicism, and a rigidly hierarchical social organization culminating in hereditary aristocracy. In Maurras's version, this was coloured by hostility towards the Jew. Maurras articulated this position eloquently and ushered it into the new century in a copious outpouring of books, articles, and pamphlets on a range of topics: literary criticism, political theory, religion, economics, and comparative culture. It can be observed that Maurrasien inheritance provided Eliot with a dominant intellectual framework that he retained throughout his life. This is not to say that no change occurred over a career, that spanned half a century; after Maurras's condemnation by the Vatican in 1926, Eliot worked feverishly to realign the component parts of this ideology, subordinating everything to religion, as he wrote to Paul Elmer More in 1936, "I am very happy you like the essay on religion and literature." What is constant is that the political dimension that was the focal point of the Maurrasien compound was advanced in sub-rosa almost usually in Eliot. Early in his career, Eliot presented classicism to an English audience as nearly exclusively a literary preference, something easy enough to be given general ignorance of the term's full implication in France. His unwillingness to be more open was due in a large part to the fact that he was a more scrupulous thinker than Maurras himself in general and he was unsure exactly how the politics, religion, and literature necessarily entailed one another. This difficulty was exacerbated by the fact that he was trying to impose classicism on a traditionally Protestant country (a problem registered in his later reference to Anglicanism as Anglo-Catholicism). Immediately upon the Vatican's condemnation of Maurras for valuing Catholicism primarily for its political function, Eliot began taking religious instruction in the Anglican faith and was accepted into the communion the following year. Thereafter, though opposing the same antagonists, he engaged them in the name of the Christian commonwealth. Politics led Eliot to religion but he rarely acknowledged the political element that constituted a central part of what he understood (Asher, 1998: 8-9).

By the use of various images throughout his poetry, Eliot could portray the cares and wishes of modern man. Imagism was a movement

31

that appeared between 1909 and 1917. It flourished in Britain and in the United States for a brief period. Imagism had three principles," as articulated by Pound: the direct treatment of the 'thing,' whether subjective or objective; the rejection of any words that do not contribute to the presentation of the image; and composition in the sequence of a musical phrase not in a sequence of a metronome" (T. E. Hulme, 1955: 74). As part of the modernist movement, away from the sentimentality and moralizing tone of the nineteenth-century Victorian poetry, imagist poets used a new technique to help them create a new poetic expression. The imagists studied and were influenced by the French symbolists, who were experimenting with free verse (*vers libre*); a verse form that used a cadence that mimicked natural speech rather than the accustomed rhythm of metrical feet, or lines. Rules of rhyming were also considered nonessential. Pound, however, was the primary theorist. The main principle involved, modeled in part on the Japanese haiku, was that the image was not to be "described" but created with precision and brevity (Miller, 2005:270). In *A Few Don'ts* by an Imagiste published in *Poetry* in March 1913, Pound defined the Image as "that which presents an intellectual and emotional complex in an instant of time" (Miller, Ibid).

The early beginning of the twentieth century Poets in all countries, employed imagism to enhance their expression and create a greater impact on the reader. Kristian Smidit has defined poetry in this way:

> Poetry is the language of actual thought, or actual ideas. Its actuality is not merely contingent and does not merely lie in its faithfulness to an external subject matter: it resides far more in its faithfulness to the movements of the mind and the spirit of the poet, which manifested in the poetic use of imagery. For actual thought, also tends to move in images (Smidit, 1961: 110).

This definition indicates that imagery is inseparable from poetry. The image that is used here is a mental picture. Imagists decided to give up the Romantic mode of expression. An Imagist anthology was published in 1914 that collected works by William Carlos Williams, Richard Aldington, and James Joyce, as well as Hilda Doolittle and Pound. By the time the anthology appeared, Amy Lowell had effectively appropriated Imagism and was seen as the movement's leader. Three

years later, even Amy Lowell thought the movement had run its course. Pound by then was claiming that he invented Imagism to launch H.D.'s career. Though Imagism as a movement was over by 1917, the ideas about poetry embedded in the Imagist doctrine profoundly influenced free verse poets throughout the twentieth century. Imagism was a reaction against the flabby abstract language and "careless thinking" of Georgian Romanticism. Imagist poetry aimed to replace muddy abstractions with exactness of observed detail, apt metaphors, and economy of language. For example, Pound's *In a Station of the Metro* started from a glimpse of beautiful faces in a dark subway and elevated that perception into a crisp vision by finding an intensified equivalent image. The metaphor provokes a sharp, intuitive discovery in order to get at the essence of life. The movement sprang from ideas developed by T.E. Hulme, who as early as 1908 was proposing to the Poets' Club in London poetry based on absolutely accurate presentation of its subject with no excess of meaningless words. The first tenet of the Imagist manifesto was "To use the language of common speech, but to employ always the exact word, not the nearly-exact, nor the merely decorative word." Images made poetry to be understood by the readers clearly; but for Eliot, the use of images and symbols made his poetry obscure and difficult. Hugh Kenner called Eliot *The invisible poet*, but the quality of using images made his poetry attractive. Changes that took place in the twentieth century affected both form and content of poetry; in terms of form the French symbolist poets offered Eliot "urban life" and "vers libre", (Thorne, 2006: 287). The poet turns away from decadent Romantic tradition. Eliot sees life in realism and the most commonplace subjects are considered suitable for the modern life. In his essay *"Tradition and the Individual Talent"*, Eliot states that it is not the duty of the poet to create a beautiful world. The poet should try to see beneath both beauty and ugliness to see the horror, boredom and glory (Tiwari, 2001:1-4).

It is possible to divide Eliot's poetry into three phases. The first, period includes those poems, which express the disillusionment of the post World War I, the second covers the period of his conversion to Anglicanism in 1927, in which he struggles with the intellectual difficulties of the religious faith, and the final period is a period with a large gap in his writing of nearly 15 years. This period ends with the "Four Quartets". The modern readers might say, "This is Eliot's solution to the problems of modern life, but I can be neither a classist nor a royalist nor a converter to Anglo-Catholicism. For such a reader the early works will almost certainly be more rewarding" (Walsh, 2007:175).

In his book, *The Durable Satisfactions of Life*, Charles, Eliot William says that the modern man in the twentieth century has hardly had any appreciation for religion, especially for Christianity. The modern mind craves an immediate motif and leads well for today. The new religion builds on the actual experiences of men, women and of human society as a whole (Eliot, 1910: 197).

It is said that the past is always an essential part of the present. The psychological weaknesses and experiences of ancients are substantially similar to those of the modern's. Eliot believed that modern man should return to the classical masters like, Homer and Dante (Cuddy, 2000: 21). Thorne comments that Eliot's interest in the works of the French Symbolists was because of their belief that it was impossible to use the conventional language to express feelings as the nineteenth century poets actually faced such kind of a problem. Eliot believed that the poet should create a special language of symbols that suggests the vague nature of experience to the reader in which a direct statement or description cannot represent real experience, but they believed that only a succession of images could convey the true meaning of consciousness. Imagists who are very direct and objective and they focused on the concrete rather than the abstract. Eliot tries to convey the essence of life rather than escaping from grinding nature of reality. Eliot's images function in a different way, which often take on a symbolic significance (Thorne, 2006: 279-280).

Eliot, who was trained in classics, was described as a man of keen intellect, capable of developing a philosophical aspect in his poetry, which is a new way of writing poetry. It has also been confirmed that he was better equipped than any other poet to bring verse fully into the twentieth century. James Joyce remarked of Eliot in a notebook that he abolished the idea of poetry for ladies; by this he gave modern poetry one of its most distinctive features (Ellmann and O'Clair, 1988: 479). Many critics and scholars refer to Eliot's philosophical training when reading his poetry. The symbols, which Eliot used are not easy for the readers to understand therefore, they connect his poetry with philosophy. There is no doubt that there are ways in which his interests in ideas have influenced his poetry. Deutch and Flam believe that some study of the primitive life is needed in order to understand modern man; so "some study of primitive man furthers our understanding of civilized man" (Deutch and Flam, 2003: 122) The wide variety of interpretations of how those ideas are actually presented in his poetry suggests that perhaps poetry was not the preferred medium for the elaboration of his thinking. One could declare that philosophy is far more important to his prose, both his critical works and his cultural criticism. Poetry, for Eliot, was the means through which he worked out the practical consequences of action and faith (Cooper, 2006: 28).

Modern man has been described as a person who voyages in the sea of life, and never stops. The journey differs from one person to another but there is no doubt about his being a seeker of his rights and perhaps true identity in his society. This does not mean that everyone can succeed in reaching his destination, because social or fatal obstacles are in front of him (Tiwari, 2001: 21).

The process of transition of human life from one stage to another means giving up the old life and starting a new one, often leading to a feeling of alienation, estrangement from the previous state. These transitions naturally differ from one individual to another, depending on the surrounding circumstances and personal understanding of what is happening. As an expatriate, his psychological, social and religious concerns made these developments in Eliot's poetry inevitable. E. M. Forster wrote of Eliot's religion, "what he seeks is not revelation but stability." The quest for psychological stability is central in Eliot's works. The social and personal agony of *The Waste Land* and the individual agony of Prufrock are responses to the instability of the modern world (Schmidt, 1979: 125-126).

Eliot's poetry holds the mirror up to the modern urban complex culture. It portrays the post-industrial image of modern man; therefore, to understand Eliot means understanding the spirit of modernism (Sarker.2008: 1). The great influence of Eliot on the poetry of the twentieth century according to Sheila Sullivan "for good or ill . . . has been immeasurable". After the publication of *The Love Song of J. Alfred Prufrock* in 1917 and *The Waste Land* in 1922, it was no longer possible for any poet to write in the manner of the Georgians. His poetry emerged exactly matching the manner to the intention, and from the beginning, his touch was lethal to the Georgian style. With Pound and Laforgue behind him, Eliot created a revolution in modern poetry (Sullivan, 1973: III).

Eliot believed that the role of the poet was to bring order to the irregular, fragmentary experience of life, transmuting ideas into sensations and amalgamating disparate experience. This belief was to make his poems into a sequence of cinematic images, which represent his own view of the world. He also believed that poets should find ways to express implicitly without using romantic outpouring of feelings or sentimentality. Thorne says Eliot believed that the only way of expressing emotion in the form of art, is by finding an "objective correlative", i.e., a set of objects, a situation and a chain of events which shall be the formula of that particular emotion; that means, when the external facts, which must terminate sensory experience, are given, the emotion is immediately evoked (Thorne, 2006: 282).

Eliot's response to the tormenting complexity of his age, which was continually modified and renewed as he suffered and matured, is a response to the immense panorama of futility and anarchy which contemporary history was essentially moral and spiritual. His principal purpose in life as a poet and man of letters was to find a way of controlling and ordering, of giving shape and significance to the chaotic fragmentation and alienation of the life of modern man. He thought that the overriding problem of modern man i.e., alienation which was the result of anarchic individualism and scientific regimentation, could be solved merely at the religious level of man's spiritual existence. Because the requisite outlook can grow only out of religion, which comprehends the entire aspects of life and effectively counteracts the futility and anarchy of contemporary social life, Eliot believed that only in the realms of religion and art the problems of the modern society can be solved (Singh, 2001: 267). There are different viewpoints among the critics of Eliot's poetry, for instance Mishra, in his book, *The Poetry of T. S. Eliot*, states that Dutta Roy's thesis, which studies the meaning of Eliot's poetry, mistakenly says that in art and poetry God is at the centre of Eliot's poetry. He is against this and states that Eliot has placed man at the centre of his poetry (Mishra, 2003: 18).

It is said that curiosity and wariness about language and culture emerge very early in Eliot's intellectual life. It is seen in the comments and observations he wrote during his university years and in his doctoral thesis, *Knowledge and Experience in the Philosophy of F. H. Bradley* (1916). But this focus on language took its most important form, not from his philosophical studies intrinsically, but in his poetry and in his criticism. The causes of this turn to language in the twentieth century are many and complex but perhaps the most important reason for a poet, the one that captures the mood of Eliot's early and even some of his late poetry, has been described best by the German philosopher Heidegger in his comments about the despoiling of language as a vital medium for connection in modern times. He argues that in modernity,

> Language in general is worn out and used up as an indispensable but master less means of communication that may be used as one pleases, as indifferent as a means of public transport, as a street car which everyone rides in. Everyone speaks and writes away in the language, without hindrance and above all without danger (Heidegger, 1961: 42)

Cooper says that Heidegger continues to say that only "a very few" of the poets are cable of bringing language back to life from the death-in-life into which it has fallen in modern times. This is the special task of poets and Eliot seems to have understood this as his own particular poetic task. The possibilities of making poetry from a fallen language, a language exhausted by use, "worn down by the non-stop tracing pedestrian chatter and triteness, was suggested by his reading of the poetry of Charles Baudelaire and Jules Laforgue" (Cooper, 2006: 41).

CHAPTER TWO

Prufrock as a Representative of the Modern Man in *The Love Song of J. Alfred Prufrock* (1917)

The Love Song of J. Alfred Prufrock (from now on *The Love Song* is used) was composed over the period 1909-1911 in Munich, Germany (Raffel, 1982: 24). It was published in June 1917 in the collection of poems called *Prufrock and Other Observations*. Eliot was fond of prefacing his poems with epigraphs from different writers, and in each case, the epigraph was designed to form an integral part of connotation of the poem. In *The Love Song,* the epigraph has been taken from Dante's *Inferno*, which presents the situation of a character that was called upon to reveal himself (Batra, 2001: 34). Eliot, in his poem was able to create a persona, which is used as a formal device to create of the formal allusiveness and resonance of the poetic language, and as a zone of "consciousness"; a moral I that takes form only through the substance of the poem's language. In the poem, the "character", Prufrock, retains upon experience of a highly weakened order, "an ironic hold, which is continuously in the process of being displaced by language". Eliot's early work dwells in this uncertainty, and it is his ability, to sustain this almost impossible dwelling between two worlds, the real world and the world of Dante's character, Guido da Montefeltro, which is hell, that constitutes his genius at this period (Grant, 1982: 3). There is a contrast between the serious epigraph from Dante's Inferno and the lighter love song of Prufrock's. In fact, the mixture of levity and seriousness is to be found throughout the whole poem. However, the epigraph is not part of the poem, but it cannot be ignored, since it highlights the significance and connotations of the poem. George Williamson believes that the first rule of reading one of Eliot's poems is to consider the possibilities suggested by the title and the epigraph of the poem (Williamson, 1953: 57-58).

The human condition is central to Eliot's depiction of the twentieth-century life. The individuals in his poems are detached from a living spiritual community and therefore despairing. In *The Love Song*, one can see the individuals searching for a pattern, for something that will give the fixity, something that will order their lives. They can be seen as the representatives of modern man (Thorne, 2006: 283). There are constant modifications of emotions and thoughts; moving from half-comic expressions of regret and nostalgia to cruel or impersonal observations could only be seen in *The love Song* (Shucard etal, 1989: 99).

Carl states in his book, *The Columbia History of British Poetry* that,

> Eliot's *The Love Song of J. Alfred Prufrock* is considered by many critics as his first masterpiece. It is already, cinematic: image and juxtaposition. Prufrock is, however belatedly, one of Nietzsche's nineteenth-century young men, his moral and religious spine broken by the say-so weight of history (Carl, 1994: 569).

In several ways, the poem is modernist in terms of its thought, which describes a melting pattern of conceptions, connected with some submerged principles of organization, working beneath consciousness. *Prufrock*'s images are drawn from both life and culture. "A model of the mind is implied in the structure of the poem, which, like the mind, is mood-driven and picks up on perceptions and cultural artifacts, reforming them into new meanings." Prufrock has intense feelings of inadequacy and is unable to express himself. The title emphasizes Prufrock's sense of insecurity. Prufrock's preoccupation with himself mirrors the anguishes faced by the individual in the modern world, which shows that the crisis of the self is also a crisis in discourse (Childs, 2000:101). Eliot discussed the ideas in *The Love Song* philosophically because when he visited Paris, he was influenced by the works of the relativist philosopher, Henri Bergson, who has influenced Eliot in writing *The Love Song* (McGowan, 2004: 64).

Eliot confessed to his brother that he was afraid of *The Love Song* to be his "swan's song", but with the publication of *The Waste Land* in 1922, his fear diminished, which made Eliot renowned as a quite prominent modernist poet (Miller, 2006: 114). The sense of duplicity within the modern man is a major motif in Eliot's *The Love Song* where the hero, Prufrock, is helplessly caught in an interminable conflict between his own desire to live by himself and the obligation to submit to the social conventions. Forbes insisted that Eliot's attempts at self-analysis are "falsifying" while Eliot's implicit analysis of his poem's character (Prufrock) is authentic, (Forbes, 2004: 94). It should not be forgotten that Eliot had never had much faith in his fellow humans. His earlier poems prove this fact; it is clear in his earlier poems, especially in *The Love Song*, that is a vivid testament to his state of mind even before the war began (Miller, 2006: 115).

The name of J. Alfred Prufrock is mentioned only in the poem's title. On the one hand, it seems to be a noble name, with the initial "J.", but on the other hand, Alfred is a very common name, and as Palmer points out the name "Prufrock" used to appear in an advertisement in St. Louis Missouri, Eliot's hometown. It was stated that behind the surface of Prufrock's name, in the tension between the nobleness suggested by the use of "J" and the common "Alfred Prufrock" the image of the speaker's self is not obvious; it is rather hidden in some place of inbetweenness. Ayers points out that the critic Hugh Kenner commented that J. Alfred Prufrock, is a name plus a voice, and rightly argued that Prufrock is not a character such as those found in one of the dramatic monologues of Tennyson or Browning (Ayers, 2004:18). Prufrock presents the picture of the speaker's self, which is lost in the surrounding environment. The reader's understanding of Prufrock's self is not obvious; either Prufrock is a noble character or a common character (Palmer, 1996: 19-20). The title is ironic, for Prufrock is timid and spiritually numb. He is a man unable to love, so no one sings **the love song**. Images of movement are juxtaposed with images of paralysis, which reflect Prufrock's internal conflict (Rozakis, 1999: 278).

The Love Song is a song of frustration and emotional conflict. This poem is composed as a dramatic monologue, traditionally a lyric poem that reveals the soul of the speaker. Many modern poets have rejected the form because of its connection with the poet Robert Browning and other Victorian poets who used the same style and technique extensively;

the modern poets thought that Browning and the Victorians represent a world of lies, which the moderns sought to escape (Miller, 2006: 126). The speaker of the poem is "I", which seems to be Prufrock. There are different viewpoints concerning the speaker and the listener; some critics think that the listener or the companion (you) is probably a woman, but others think that the "you and I" of the first line can be interpreted as two parts of Prufrock's personality. One part urges him to participate in the experience, but the other part holds him back (Kaplan, 1997:18). The first line of the poem is written in the form of a debate between "you" and "I". The title suggests a friend, a lady, but according to George Williamson, the epigraph suggests "a scene out of the world, on a submerged level". Is the "I" giving into a lady? Is going to a more acceptable rendezvous? Alternatively, is he submissive for the moment to an urgent "you" with whom he is not in harmony? (Williamson, 1953: 59).

Kristian Smidt, in his book, *Poetry and Belief in the Work of T. S. Eliot* that was first published in English in 1961 and appeared originally in Norwegian in 1949, wrote to Eliot enquiring as to the identity of the companion accompanying the title character in *The Love Song*. Eliot wrote in his letter of reply,

> As for *"The Love Song of J. Alfred Prufrock"*, anything I say now must be somewhat conjectural, as it was written so long ago that my memory may deceive me; but I am prepared to assert that the "you" in *The Love Song,* is merely some friend or companion, presumably of the male sex, whom the speaker is at that moment addressing and that it has no emotional content whatever (Smidt, 2002: 85).

This somewhat ambiguous comment, with what appears to be a defensive conclusion, needs to be placed beside another comment that Eliot made about "Prufrock" later in a 1962 interview in *Granite Review*, where, he says, "Prufrock" was partly a dramatic creation of a man of about 40 . . . and partly an expression of feeling of my own. I always feel that dramatic characters that seem living creations have something of the author in them", (Miller, 2005:3-4). What Eliot said, implies that it is possible to connect Prufrock with the poet himself. Like Prufrock, Eliot has faced many problems in his life and like this character of his poem Eliot tried hard to solve his problems in the modern society. The world of the poem is not a serious one, but it is rather a trivial world like that of Alexander Pope's *The Rape of the Lock*, a world where people spent their time with playing cards and the tea parties were one of the most significant events that can be a sort of comfort and relief for them. It is obvious that the connection between the speaker of Dante's epigraph and Prufrock is that, although it is in an earthly situation similar to hell, Prufrock is still worried about his honour. His negative concept of honour consists of not being laughed at as "the Fool" (Cervo, 2002: 207). A. D. Moody, in his book *Thomas Stearns Eliot: Poet*, suggests a similarity of the situation between Prufrock and Guido. Both are in hell. Prufrock finds himself in a situation, in a society, which is like hell for him, and believes, like Guido, that there is no way out. One should never ignore the epigraph in Eliot because it gives hints of the meaning or the message of the poem (Moody, 1979: 37). Because of the significance of the epigraph in *The Love Song*, many critics have rightly directed the attention of the reader to the epigraph:

> If I believed that my reply would be to someone, whoever would return to the world this flame would wag no more. But because what I hear, if be true no one ever does return alive from this depth I reply to you without fear of infamy (Ward, 1973: 13).

The speaker of this epigraph is from hell who gives his reason why he is freely speaking without any fear of scandal. He thinks that nobody is listening to him who could ever possibly return from hell to the world. Miller says that the epigraph introduces the theme of paralysis and constraint. The speaker of those lines, Guido da Montefeltro, is encased within a flame in hell, unable to escape. Prufrock is paralyzed in another sort of hell, the hell of the modern city, within which his social group is equally disapproving (Miller, 2006: 126).

In his book, *The American T. S. Eliot*, Eric Sigg affirms that Eliot depicts the duplicity between the character his environment, and between the "warning elements within a single soul." This duplicity makes Prufrock suffer helplessly. The two selves that are the personal and the social, have to tolerate each other, for treating each self, Prufrock, however, has some strategies to the common people. Prufrock, the representative of the modern man, has a different self to put forward. This self, as Eliot expresses, was something artificial that should be prepared: "There will be time; there will be time to prepare a face to meet the faces that you meet" (Lines, 26-27). This notion may imply that man, in order to be accepted by others, tries to make himself as similar to them as possible. Joseph Conrad strikes the idea even further. He states, "We can at times be compelled into a mysterious recognition of our opposite as our true self" (Abrams, etal, 2000: 847). When man lives in a society, he must cope himself with all the difficulties he faces there. When he cannot cope with the delicate situations he might then feel sad then his sadness may become a kind of alienation, which means he must solve the problems by himself. It is clear that one cannot face all of his daily problems unless there is one to help him. Finally man can only pose questions without any one's answer and he may face psychological trauma in his life. If he did not share his feelings with the other people who reside in the same society his problems will never be solved.

Northrop Frye had established romance as an archetype. Eliot has handled this archetype of romance between man and woman. Eliot's poem *The Love Song* presents a similar situation to Northrop Frye's *Theory of archetype*. Prufrock is a middle-aged man who was in love with a young woman. He wants to declare his love to her; therefore, Prufrock makes a journey and tries to establish a harmonious relationship with the woman he loves. The first line of the poem is a hint at the beginning of the journey (Tiwari, 2001: 22).

By the use of imagery and allusions, Eliot is able to represent the triviality of Prufrock's life and his lack of self-confidence, which symbolically stand, not only for Prufrock and the society he lives in, but also for the twentieth century society and its life. The use of allusions, in *The Love Song*, puts the sort of demands on its readers that later modernist poems like *The Waste Land* and *The Cantos* would greatly intensify. In order to fully grasp the poem, the reader must recognize and place in a new context a number of literary and Biblical allusions, including Dante's *Inferno*, Shakespeare's *Hamlet*, Marvell's *To His Coy Mistress*, Hesiod's *Works and Days*, and the stories of Lazarus and John the Baptist. Further, Eliot's use of imagery, diction, and figurative language contribute to a style utterly different from that of any previous

American poem and with a wise arrangement of the technique of his poem he could depict the image of modern man (Beach, 2003: 38).

The choice of words in the poem's title, *The Love Song* creates a specific atmosphere that helps Eliot to convey the main aim of his *song*, which is love. The poet opens his text for discussion with this particular title, which can be interpreted as a joke. The connection between the title and the rest of the text is not explicit; but by introducing the text as a love song, Eliot opens it to certain expectations, which are followed by further conversations between the speaker and the reader, as in the lines:

> "Let us go then you and I,
> When the evening is spread out against the sky"
> (lines 1 and 2)

No doubt this does not mean that the reader is able to provide true, definite answers to the questions posed by Prufrock, which are mostly open questions, like, if he dares to "disturb the universe" by talking to others and "how he should begin" his communication with women. These questions lie behind his overwhelming quest for meaning of existence and his quest for love:

> "To lead you to an overwhelming question . . .
> Oh do not ask, what "what is it?"
> Let us go and make our visit." (Lines, 10-13)

This should be a warning to the reader that only knowledge of literary tradition will not help them understand the poem completely. Rather, traditional literary forms will be brought together in the poem to make a new form; a form that is perhaps more relevant to addressing the concerns of the modern world (Miller, 2006: 130). Though Eliot deliberately made his poems very complex yet he was successful to make the reader understand his poems. He was able to depict the image of modern man, which is complex one like his poetry, probably the reason behind making his poetry uneasy is to show life as meaningless, sterile and people in the modern life are only busy for the materialistic things as if they live in a Godless universe.

It can be suggested that the main goal of choosing this specific title for the poem is to convey its influences on the reader rather than its meanings. These influences place both the reader and the speaker in the mental landscape of love, which is partly placed among the living people; when, for example, the speaker invites the reader to "the room where the woman come and go/ Talking of Michaelangelo," and partly among the dead, where human voices wake him, and he drowns." The problem is that Prufrock finds his meaning neither among the living nor among the dead; his meaning is to be found somewhere else, in the liminal world of "inbetweenness", where the "mermaids sing each to each." Looking at the title, the reader expects to find some thoughts of love in the lines, which follow. In order to understand what love means for Prufrock and where the answers can be found, the reader is supposed to find his own space of understanding, where a new area is being created, where his or her understanding fuses with Prufrock's, in a fusion of horizons. This is the space where, on the one hand, the reader's and the speaker's insight may mingle with each other, and, on the other hand, where Prufrock's horizon of understanding, perhaps finds an opportunity to merge with the other people's. It is pointed out that, when *The Love Song* is read for the first time, it has to be scrutinized for it possesses two stylistic features that need understanding: the fragmentary effect of the poem, which modern life offers and the subliminal awareness of the allusions to other literary works, which may raise certain readerly anxiety. The modern man is thus, fragmentary; the sense of harmony and congruity are missing in their life. Prufrock covers precisely the period of Eliot's migration from USA to Europe; i.e., a physical migration via France to Britain, but what is more important is an intellectual migration of the intellectual people to Europe because it became a centre where they could meet to and share their knowledge (Brown and Gupta, 2005: 236-238). The problems of the modern man are so intense that makes love meaningless. It can be argued that the trauma and dilemma of the modern man are numerous that not only *The Love Song* has never been sung and even the lover forgets that he loves a lady because of the overwhelming questions, which were not answered by any one. Perhaps Prufrock thinks that in dead society, there is not any healthy individual and furthermore, one can only think of death and the other problems rather than his own private problems. Eliot could portray the image as it was.

Eliot by juxtaposing fragments of voices, images, and scenes constructs the image of modern man, which evokes the desperate inner life of a speaker. The poem itself suggests that the character of Prufrock is psychologically unbalanced, anti-hero, whose indecision and excess of his self-consciousness wasting his time in his efforts to express his feelings and also to approach the woman he desires (Bloom, 1999: 18). It is said that *The Love Song* may be made up, in terms of stanza, of poetic forms that were traditionally used for love-songs and that was used by Michelangelo in his rhyme (Leisi, etal, :173). There is a clue to show that Prufrock a hesitant, fearful, indecisive character in the poem, which indicates that modern men are also like Prufrock. They cannot do anything except for wasting time and thinking that the rest of the other people are gazing at him and criticizing them for their physical appearance while in reality the opposite is true. When Prufrock is psychologically unbalanced like Hamlet and is doubtful of whether he can do anything in his life, he cannot solve his problems like Hamlet that is why he says I am not like Hamlet and do not want to be like him.

The imagery in the first fourteen lines of the poem establishes the atmosphere of the modern life, which is disillusionment and passivity that spreads through the poem. The conceit in which the speaker makes a comparison between the evening and an "etherized patient" is not like the reader's expectations about the lyrical landscape, but offers instead a sterile image of an urban landscape, which appears inimical to human life. Many things in the poem show the speaker's sense of isolation and frustration like, "half-deserted streets". The speaker seems to offer another form of mindless escape, another possibility for numbing himself to the alienation and isolation he is feeling (Miller, 2006: 123). He should have been born a crab, a creature without emotions, and a "scuttling" bottom feeder of the ocean. Prufrock's self-loathing is apparent in these lines:

> "I should have been a pair of ragged claws
> Scuttling across the floors of silent seas" (Lines, 72-73).

Although he tries to retreat into these lonely avenues, they seem to be "muttering" to him as if reminding him of his unpleasant situations that he cannot escape from them (Lawrence etal, 1985: 320).

Tomichan, Matheikal points out that the man who is incapable of making a commitment is the patient who sleeps under the effect of ether at the beginning of the poem. He also believes that the external objects are seen by Prufrock as the extension of Prufrock's own self. The evening is also an extension of Prufrock's self; it is mentioned after Prufrock expresses his helpless desire to escape from his consciousness. The weariness of the evening is Prufrock's weariness. He lacks "the strength to force the moment to its crisis," which is the capitulation of the self (Matheikal, 2003: 124). Harold Bloom says that the reader's expectation of romantic reverie is quickly undercut by the horrible image of "a patient etherized upon a table", (Bloom, 1999: 18) when the reader knows the time of going, he will also know where to go, through a cheap district of the town, (Batra, 2001: 36).

Eliot in *The love Song* depicts a trivial, sordid and empty world. In fact, it begins with a highly selective scene which establishes the character of Prufrock incidentally. The poem shows that Eliot was aware of the problem and dilemma of modern man. The hollowness and boredom of modern man have resulted in a sense of loss and disgust: "With the third line of *The Love Song*, the romantic mood set by the opening couplet collapses, and modern poetry begins" (Brehm, 2006: 342).

The lines 1-5 show the metaphysical concept of the poem that reflects the tone of the poem immediately. Comparing the evening to a patient etherized upon a table establishes the tone and setting of the poem. Eliot suggests that Prufrock and evening are identical, both of them are peaceful, but with a suggestion of unhealthiness and absence of importance. It is noticeable here that the outward scene does not exist. The next image is also important because it emphasizes the impression of disease and helplessness:

> "Let us go through certain half-deserted streets,
> The muttering retreats
> Of restless nights of one-night cheap hotels . . . .
> Streets that follow like a tedious argument
> Of insidious intend
> To lead you to an overwhelming question" (Lines, 4-9).

The phrase "one-night cheap hotels" suggests the sense of loss and the homelessness of the human soul. There is something common between Prufrock and "streets that follow like a tedious argument." Both are unstable and shifting. The streets will lead nowhere and similarly the reflections of Prufrock are torturous and endless (Batra, 2001: 45).

Then, Eliot compares the fog, to a cat in its movement, 'The yellow fog that rubs its back upon the window panes." And "Prufrock himself is unable to love neither a woman nor love. His narcissism is a plastic suit in which he pretends to be ill, sweating a dull mental disorder. Nothing touches him, and he will not touch anything except for the imaginary fog lying like a cat beside his chair" (Carl, 1994: 570). This image is very significant, as it corresponds to certain emotional realities. By some other images like "the voices dying with a dying fall" and "the eyes that fix you in formulated phrase" and other images, the poet attempts to draw the basic outline of an image of the modern man, represented by Prufrock in the poem. This image, which is drawn from the contemporary world, is not merely decorative; it is an integral part of the poem and helps Eliot to present the peculiar situation in which Prufrock finds himself. Eliot dramatizes the condition of the modern man in terms of tragedy and comedy by establishing the kinship of Prufrock with the scene of the evening (Batra, 2001: 45-46). Prufrock is the image of a man who is too fastidious to trust his instincts, and is hesitant, but he is not as tragic as Hamlet. The image of the cat signifies that even the animals have been affected by the sense of loss. The cat does not know what to do as if, it is left by itself, and it is in search of finding its partner. The fog, then, represents the hopelessness of a limited vision, a vision limited by fixed ways of thinking and feeling, so that the more he might squirm or might conspire to escape the enclosed social space within which he feels himself trapped, "pinned and wriggling" under both imagined and real evaluative gazes, the more he becomes exposed.

The poem concerns Prufrock's visiting a woman, and his inability to reveal his love to her mirrors the modern man's inability to communicate. He believes that the woman would have rejected his proposal by saying, "That is not it at all, /That is not what I meant, at all", unable to force the moment to its climax, Prufrock asks "Do I dare?", and "Should I then presume?" He resigns himself to be a monitor player an "attendant lord" doomed to flutter on the fringes of life. The physical world of Prufrock is the urban streets. Modifiers like, half-deserted, restless and tedious suggest the disorder of the modern life. It seems that Prufrock is in a world where he cannot say what he wants to say, thus his tone is marked by failure. It is pointed out that the use of modal would repeatedly; reveal Prufrock's inability to act implicitly (Thorne, 2006: 283-284). References to detached body parts like, face, hands, voices, eyes, and arms intensify the loss of humanity by reducing individuals to fragments. It is clear that Prufrock sees himself in terms of his bald spot, his arms, legs, and his clothes; which denotes hypocrisy. He is not connected to his inner self and his image viewed from above on the stairs becomes an objective correlative for the division of self that disallows meaningful action in modern society. For Eliot, nothing is complete and these symbols represent the human condition in the modern world.

Eliot completely rejects discursive poetry: "one cannot ask what it means, but can only ask what it *is*". The answer to this kind of a question is only general: the poem, which attempts to project and universalize a state of modern man's mind, is Eliot's *The Love Song*. To know better what it is, one must know about the influence of Laforgue on Eliot, which is "an art of the nerves, and it is what all art would tend towards if one followed his nerves on all his journeys. "Unlike Eliot, Laforgue can be arrogantly sexual. His poetry is close to sex-puns. He is much more frank than Eliot," (Oser, 2007: 47) C. K. Stead states that Eliot followed his nerves in the following lines:

> "It is impossible to say just what I mean!
> But as if a magic lantern threw the nerves in
> Patterns on a screen" (Lines, 126-128).

Prufrock is tormented by his inability to love and communicate the suffocating environment of the closed rooms and narrow streets (Stead, 1964: 155). His incapability to break out his isolation and his acute self-consciousness of the universe is seen in these lines when he asks:

> "Do I Dare?
> To disturb the universe?
> In a minute, there is time for decisions and revisions
> Which a minute will reverse." (Lines, 47-50)

Eliot's heroes do not succeed to confront their own selfhood from the beginning, whether this is conceived as Dantesque *Heart of light* or Conradian *Heart of darkness*, because Prufrock at the beginning of the poem shows timidness and does not dare to make his visit (Moody, 1994: 111). It is seen that Prufrock carefully shows himself as modest, fashionable and sociable but he also reveals his self-consciousness about what others say about him, like: "how his hair is growing thin!" and "how his arms and legs are thin!". What helps Eliot to compose *Prufrock* is Dante, Michaelangelo, Shakespeare, Dostoevsky, and the Bible. (Sanders, 1999: 532-533)

Man is instinctively and naturally a creature different from how he appears in the public. It is obvious, for example, in his being bored with his fellowmen as soon as they try to penetrate to his personal life. In this sense, man is a hypocrite, and a double dealer. Man has a sense of duplicity regarding his own self. He suffers in the society yet he is unable to do something to change it. Derek Traversi in his book, *T. S. Eliot: The Longer Poems*, states that the modern man is the cause of the corruption in society; it is not the society which corrupts modern man. According to Traversi, Man is psychologically handicapped. He is unable to take the necessary actions (Traversi, 1976: 22-28). Loss of privacy is another aspect of the modern life which had a strong negative impact on the way modern perceives life. Man needs to have his privacy and secrets kept, but when others try to know about his secrets he may resort to hypocrisy and does not show his real character. To change hypocrisy in the modern society man needs to have his privacy kept. When he was not sure of his private life, he may no more participate in the society and even become completely absent.

Hugh Kenner in his *The Invisible Poet* argues that the conflict between Prufrock, who stands for the modern man and his personal problems with society "condemns him (Prufrock) to boredom and passivity." He considers modern man's role in society no more than that of a fool (Line, 20). The fact is expressed explicitly in the poem where Prufrock is analyzing himself as: "At times, indeed, almost ridiculous. / Almost, at times, the Fool" (lines 118-119). As a result of this view, Prufrock retreats to his own self, which would result in a problem: his inability to communicate, which leads consequently to a sense of isolation that is a basic theme of *The Love Song*. The idea, which is presented by Martin Scofield, in *T. S. Eliot: The Poems*, emphasizes the relationship between a man and a woman. Prufrock seems to be unable to communicate with those who are around him, men and women. However, it seems that others are equally unable to have a positive relation with him. Thus, inability to communicate is a common problem, but the problem of Prufrock is that he is aware of this fact; others are not and this exacerbates his problem. Although it seems that others are having conversations as:

> "In the room the women come and go,
> Talking of Michelangelo" (Lines 13-14 and 35-36).

But "talking about Michelangelo would be a kind of escape each speaker resorts to that sort of conversation, in order not to be touched by the other person's real words about the real life situation". That kind of talking about Michelangelo, in other words, is not a genuine communication since it does not penetrate to real people's life. When Prufrock cannot sing the love song, it is not simply an irony, but it is part of the specifications of failure. Rajan argues that if Prufrock were able to sing, it would mean he will achieve a definition but his fate falls short of definition, to bring significant news to the thresholds in the future events (Rajan, 1976: 8).

Prufrock is not supposed to be a prophet, "I am no prophet—and here is no great matter" (Line, 83). As Ledbetter James points out "Prufrock renounces his inherited, romantic role as poet as prophet and renounces poetry's role as a successor to religion", (Ledbetter, 1992: 41) or as John the Baptist, or a hero like Hamlet, who seeks to answer his overwhelming question: "To be or not to be?" Eliot's character rather tries to find an explanation and a reason for the meaninglessness of life. For Prufrock, to be among the dead or living does not play a decisive role; the only thing he wishes to obtain is harmony within himself, which can be achieved through the harmony with women; assuming this harmony as a need, a basis for his search for love. *The Love Song* is, in brief, a passionately ironic poem, prepared to show the reader the human potential of sterile socialites like Prufrock at a time and simultaneously the immutably helpless nature of that sterility. This is affecting him even when it is painless, and "the mermaids singing, each to each." However, it remains conclusively true that "they will not sing to me." Prufrock can wonder, but he cannot dare. He can, in the style of John the Baptist, weep and pray, but "I am not prophet—and here is no great matter" (Raffel, 1982: 26-27).

Matheikal Tomichan, states that Prufrock thinks of certain great people who found meaning in life through a complete self-surrender. The line, "I have wept and fasted, wept and prayed," refers to Jesus' mental agony before submitting himself to the will of God. Prufrock compares himself to John the Baptist whose head was "brought in upon a platter." The Baptist, John was beheaded because he was committed unconditionally to a cause, which demanded surrender of the self to the natural flow of reality of that the self is a part. Such commitment may lead one to a tragic end as in the case of Jesus and John the Baptist. Eliot portrays the image of Prufrock as a person who foresees such a possible end for himself, if he makes the commitment:

> "And I have seen the eternal footman, hold my coat
>   and snicker." (Line, 86)
> Admitting his fear of this possible end, Prufrock refuses
>   to commit himself to life (Tomichan, 2003: 124).

The speaker in *The Love Song* is not just a speaker of one of Eliot's poems. He is the representative man of early Modernism, who is Shy, cultivated, oversensitive, sexually retarded (many have said impotent), ruminative, isolated, self-aware to the point of solipsism; as Prufrock says, "Am an attendant lord, one that will do / To swell a progress, start a scene or two." Nothing revealed the Victorian upper classes in Western society more accurately, until a novel was written by Henry James, and nothing better exposed the dreamy, insubstantial center of that consciousness of modern life than a half-dozen poems in Eliot's first book. The speaker of Eliot's early poems is trapped inside his own excessive alertness. Prufrock looks out on the world from deep inside private cave of feeling, and though he sees the world and himself with unflattering exactness, he cannot or will not do anything about his dilemma and finally falls back on self-serving explanation. He quakes before the world, and his only revenge is to be alert. After *The Love Song*, poetry came from the city and from the intellectual poets, rather than from the countryside. It could no longer stand comfortably on its old post-romantic ground, ecstatic before the natural world (Mayers and Wojahan, 1991: 1). The force, which drives Prufrock, is Eliot's youthful desire to fuse in his poetry his alienated erotic self, his transfixed social self, his intellectual philosophic self and his introspective artistic self, which can be seen separated out into various incompatible discourses in his early experiments in language (Rosen, 2005: 88).

In certain lines of the poem, metaphor dissolves into metonymy. The metaphor has reduced to series of metonyms, and thus it stands as a rhetorical introduction to what follows. The people in the poem also appear as disembodied parts or ghostly creatures. They are "the faces that you meet," the "hands / That lift and drop a question on your plate," the "Arms that are braceleted and white and bare," the "eyes that fix you in a formulated phrase." Prufrock himself fears such a reduction, to use Kenneth Burke's term for the effect of metonymy. The dreadful questions "How his hair is growing thin!" and "But how his arms and legs are thin" reduce Prufrock to certain body parts, the thinness of which stands for the diminution caused by the rhetorical figures (Bloom, 1999: 19).

In this poem, the horror of sex seems to come in part from its power to metonymize. Like Augustine, Eliot sees sex as the tyranny of one part of the body over the whole. Though Eliot is far too circumspect to name this part, he figures its power in his poetry by the rebelliousness of mere organs: hands, arms, eyes. Sexual desire pulls the body apart, so that to give in to it is to suffer permanent dismemberment. This may account for the odd combination in Eliot's work of sexual ennui and libidinous violence. The tyranny of one part scatters all the others, reducing the whole to impotence. In this way, the violence of sex robs the individuals. An oddly similar relationship of the part to the whole governs Prufrock's conception of time. In a burst of confidence, he asserts, "In a minute there is time / For decisions and revisions which a minute will reverse." (Lines, 47-48) Yet he seems to quail before the very amplitude of possibility contained in time, so that all these decisions and revisions are foreclosed before they can be made. Thus, Prufrock's prospective confidence in the fullness of time becomes a retrospective conviction that "I have known them and already, known them all:—/ Have known the evenings, mornings, afternoons . . . ." To know "all" already is to be paralyzed, disabled, because "all" is not full of possibility but paradoxically empty, constituted as it is by pure repetition, part on part. In the figure that exactly parallels the bodily metonymies, time becomes a collection of individual parts, just as the poem's human denizens had been little more than parts: "And I have known the eyes already, known them all"; "And I have known the arms already known them all" (Lines, 63 and 55). The instantaneous movement from part to whole, from eyes, arms, evenings, mornings, to "all," expresses the emptiness and the gap between dispersed parts and an oppressive whole made of purely serial repetition. The very reduction of human beings to their parts and of time to episodes makes it impossible to conceive of any whole different from this empty, repetitious "an." As Burke says, metonymy substitutes quantity for quality, so that instead of living, Prufrock feels "I have measured out my life with coffee spoons" (North, Michael, 2001: 77), which means that he has attempted hard in many ways to solve his problems but he could not and therefore; he is fed up and tired with life. He no longer wants to be alive in that state of mind which is no more than hesitancy.

The idea of duplicity, experienced by man, and between man and society, has a general impact on man's perception of life. Tangible communication, generally referred to, infiltrates the communicator's mind, and makes a way to their inner selves. In truth, there appears no sign of communication in the talking on Michelangelo where some women would presumably maneuver over some already-known, stereotyped talk about Michelangelo who, in his time, being an artist, is deliberately chosen by Eliot as a source of attraction to women. Thus, the scene acts as an entertaining subject to talk about. Nevertheless, the women would, as the nature of such talks importunes, concentrate on out-witting each other by putting across deeper familiarity with the artist and his works. They do not, however, involve with real conversation about their real living fellows. This might have the same cause, as Prufrock's unwillingness to reveal his thoughts and feelings. The repetition of these two lines indicates that when he says "That is not what I meant at all; That is not it, at all." There are three places in the poem where Eliot refers to the lack of communication; line 97 "Should say that is not what I mean at all" and line 98 "That is not it, at all," which is also (repeated in line 110 "That is not what I meant, at all."). "In the room the women come and go/Talking of Michaelangelo". Although the idea is similar in all of the above mentioned lines, the motives seem to be different in each of them. In lines 97 and 110, for instance, one can observe that Prufrock is uncommunicative because he fears to be misinterpreted. In the following lines his fear is seen, "It is impossible to say just what I mean!" (103), and "Full of high sentence, but a bit obtuse;" (117) however, what makes Prufrock unwilling to speak about his feelings is the simple fact that he is unable to utter his words: "Full of high sentence, but a bit obtuse" (117). The fear of being misinterpreted is basic to Prufrock's preference to be silent. This fear, as expressed in lines 97 and 110, results from consciousness on the part of Prufrock of the idea of lack of communication. In the two lines, Prufrock imagines that he would be able to break the ice and talk to someone, a woman in this case; and wonders what would be the outcome of that? Prufrock believes it to be misinterpreted by the lady: She would say: "That is not what I meant at all. That is not it, at all," which again shows the duplicity of modern man (Lines 97-98 109-110). In this way, Prufrock was mostly silent because he did not dare to start a conversation. There is also another cause for Prufrock's silence. In the lines 103 and 117, he explicitly alludes to the fact that Prufrock was unable to reveal his love for the lady he loves. In line 103, it is declared that: "It is impossible to say just what I mean!" Prufrock seems to be willing to express whatever he has in his mind. Yet, he seems devoid of the means, hence words. Eliot carries on with this idea to line 117, where he briefly and beautifully summarizes Prufrock: "Full of sentence, but a bit obtuse" (Line, 13).

Lack of communication as a theme of modern man's alienation mirrors the problem of isolation. This theme is, in fact, the central theme of Eliot's *The Love Song*. Here, Eliot tries to delineate man as a creature isolated from the community. This man is unable to be among the public. These two aspects of modern man seem to be at odds with each other. This oddity implies that human relations are futile and useless. Man should retreat to the remote distances of his mind. The poem, as a whole, affirms this idea. The poem, being a monologue, is again a symptom of Prufrock's isolation. In this sense, all the actions take place in the speaker's mind. There is no actual action. Walking "at dusk through narrow streets," and "coming from the dead," then "disturbing the universe," even such minute actions of "scuttling across the floors of silent seas" and other references to other actions were mixed in an irregular way throughout the poem, which are but fake and false actions taking place in Prufrock's imagination. He does nothing. He is isolated and far removed from the actual world to perform an action. He cannot enjoy being with others or, if he can, it will be so painful.

Others' experience is not better. G. B. Harrison, in his book *Major British Writers*, describes these people as "People whose pleasure are so sordid and so feeble that they seem almost sadder than their pains" (Harrison, 1957:830). Prufrock's isolation is reported in different ways in 'The Love Song". In a series of lines, one can observe that Prufrock considers himself as a man who stands outside the community. He looks at people as an outsider as groups, which can be seen in the following lines: "They will say: "How his hair is growing thin!" (42), "They will say: But how his legs and arms are thin!," (44), "For I have known them all, already, known them all" (49), "I have known the eyes already, known them all" (55), and in "And I have known the arms already, known them all," These lines show that the parts of the body cannot attract Prufrock's attention since he had already known them. (Batra, 2001: 10).

No one could save Prufrock from his isolation. Sexual connotations are evident that they cannot help him. The idea of isolation, however, finds a new dimension in lines 42, and 44, where, Prufrock shows himself conscious of the people around him. He believes that they look at him questioningly. They are faultfinding. The most terrible scene which is imagined by Prufrock, takes place when they begin to talk about his physical deficiencies. His hair and his arms as well as his legs are the targets of their criticism. Lines 42 and 44 read "They will say: 'How his hair is growing thin!" and "they will say: "How his arms and legs are thin!" emphasize this argument. (Line, 12) This sense of consciousness about the surroundings is described as a hindrance to understand his surroundings. This idea is affirmed by *The McGraw-Hill Guide to English Literature*, which diagnoses the case as, "the consciousness presented in the poem is an intensely anxious and important one in that the speaker is unable to draw conclusions about anything" (Line, 321). He is nervous about that. He thinks that he is under their scrutiny, which deepens his sense of isolation. He, consequently, realizes that he finds "the chambers of the sea", as the only suitable place for him to dwell in. (Line, 129) Society seems to have a share in Prufrock's sense of isolation, yet, Prufrock seems to be responsible for his sufferings. That is because everything happens within him. As a result, he becomes more and more alienated. The ellipses, which follow the image of the "ragged claws" in the middle of the poem, also function to represent Prufrock's suppression of painful thoughts (Lawrence, etal, 1985: 323).

Eliot's techniques in *The Love Song* are both exceedingly deft and exceedingly diverse. He owed much, as all artists do, in many directions, to the other literary figures. Too much can be made of those debts as Ezra Pound commented: "He is the only American I know who has made what I can call adequate preparation for writing" (Raffel, 1982: 28). Perhaps the most difficult aspect of this poem is what might be called "indeterminacy". Eliot is constantly making two important kinds of assumptions as to his readership: first, that his readers can understand his allusions, his references to people and to literary works, and second, that his readers can readily reconstruct an entire skeleton as it was presented. "Eliot's allusions are not much of a problem in *"Prufrock,"* though they become a matter of some importance later on in his work" (Raffel, 1982: 29-30). Perhaps the best example in *The Love Song* is the couplet towards the end, "I grow old . . . I grow old . . . / I shall wear the bottoms of my trousers rolled." Raffel analyses the above lines as something which be read in the skilful pages of Eliot's many scholarly explicators, that this description above refers to the "stylish trousers with cuffs" (Schneider Elisabeth Wintersteen, 1975: 28). Eliot could show all the aspects of the modern life in *The Love Song*. There is the fear of ageing and inability to do anything, even not to be able to have a peach, which shows that he is impotent to have close relationship with ladies that he met in different which he visited. The type of clothes he mentioned belongs to modern period and with the modern clothes he brings an old man to indicate the opposite things that can complete the meaning of the poem. The speaker is complaining against a boring life.

Indeterminacy can be confusing if not kept under control. Even in *The Love Song,* readers have been in trouble of understanding the "overwhelming question" for years, which is never clearly formulated. It is considered as a shock, such readers have argued, to shock other new readers into understanding of indeterminate metaphors like, "I have measured out my life with coffee spoons," which one cannot take them literally but they instead, oblige readers forcefully to observe the intense triviality of Prufrock's well-bred existence. The overwhelming question, which Prufrock dares not to ask, is about the absurdity of modern life; "What is the meaning of this life? Eliot realizes the boredom of his works and days, and he thinks that a more fruitful and meaningful life must exist" (Nancy Duvall Hargrove, 1978: 48). If readers of Eliot's poetry read closely enough, they will understand the poem easily, and this is what Eliot expects the readers to do. The use of perfect conditional tense in two stanzas marks a shift in Prufrock's awareness. In each stanza he repeats this line, "And would it have been worth it, after all" (Line, 6) and then takes the reader through the trivial world to the teacups and delicacies to overwhelm emotional connections of individuals. By describing his world, which is meaningless, Eliot reminds the reader that his great moment of revelation or questioning may have been mistaken by those who inhabit it. Perhaps, he had suggested that it would not be worth acting it in a world that does not appreciate either one's action or the great effort it takes to act. On the one hand, one can conclude that Prufrock has accepted his fate and has moved on to try and console himself with questions about whether it is really so bad that he was not able to act (Miller, 2006: 124). On the other hand, Roberts, Beth Ellen points out that the condition of Prufrock never changes, but it is 'we' that drowns at the end of the poem (Roberts, 2006: 92). `Comparing himself to Lazarus who rose from death, Prufrock suggests that the society he seeks to impress would dismissively assert, "That is not what I mean at all" (Line, 6). Prufrock suggests that this is not hospitable to make profound questions or enlightened observations because of their ignoring him. He answers his suppressed self because "none ever did return alive from this depth"; hence he can answer without fear of being exposed. The reasons for this suppression involve other fears. The "you" is the amorous self, the sex instinct, direct and forthright; but it is now suppressed by the timid self, finding at best evasive expression; always opposed by fear of the carnal, which motivates the defensive analogies. It is to that buried self that Prufrock addresses himself and excuses himself. Prufrock's love song is a song of being divided between passion and timidity. This song is never sung in the real world. For this poem develops a theme of frustration, of emotional conflict which is dramatized by the "you and I" (Miller, 2006: 124). It is clear that Hamlet and John the Baptist had problems in their life because of this Eliot compares Prufrock to them. The two were successful as Dante has gone through purgatory towards Paradise, where Beatrice and the meaning of life can be seen but Prufrock did not succeed because he could not encounter anything in his search for the meaning of life and also for his love. Perhaps Eliot left the meaning of life and Prufrock's love for the reader to find.

CHAPTER THREE

Tiresias as a Modern Man in "The Waste Land" (1922)

Eliot's modernist poem, *The Waste Land* was composed in the autumn of 1921 in Lausanne, Switzerland, where Eliot had gone to recuperate after a breakdown. Eliot's own remark about poetry came more easily to the mind when he felt slightly ill, or recuperating, which may be an oblique reference to his own composition of *The Waste Land.* The poem, which appeared first in the opening number of the *Criterion* in October 1922, presents itself as an alternative to the decaying society Eliot found himself inhabiting (Batra, 2001: 57-58). It begins as a personal means of pulling together one's fragmented consciousness, but in doing so, Eliot manages to present a solution to a world of selfishness, where he was looking for the problems of modern man. Through a careful study of the landscapes and urban scenes, Eliot presents the progress of his characters' fates over the course of five sections. A close look at these individuals populating *The Waste Land* will further enlighten the modern man's search for answers for the drought. Finally, Eliot's rich language will be its own ambiguous key to enlightenment, by which people critically consider the scenarios he presents. Along the way, Eliot will invoke an enormous number of literary and cultural sources to create the tale's framework, from Dante and Chaucer to Whitman and F. H. Bradley. The poet will also draw from religious traditions of the world, with a particular influence on Buddhism and Christianity to help navigate his wilderness, and the image of modern man.

Edmund Wilson considers the poem as a mirror reflecting the modern man of post-war society, with a new way in its borrowings, though he recognizes in Eliot the peculiar conflicts of the Puritan artist. Conrad Aiken, who has absorbed critics down until present day, raises the crucial question: "what kind of unity and structure does the poem have?" For Aiken, *The Waste Land*, is "a brilliant and kaleidoscopic", but the "heap of broken images" is justified "as a series of brilliant, brief, unrelated or dimly related pictures by which a consciousness empties itself of its characteristic contents". George Watson stresses the extraordinary quickness with which the poem was accepted as a masterpiece, which has a great influence on young readers. In 1930, E. M. Forster, Bonamy Dobree, William Empson, Laura Riding, and Robert Graves were among the many writers praising its virtues. Perhaps the most influential writer was, I.A. Richards, who extended his principles of literary criticism in 1926 by an appendix on T. S. Eliot. He did not find a logical scheme in *The waste Land*, but he argues that readers react with a unified emotional response. The poetry achieves form by "a music of ideas", a phrase repeatedly criticized and discussed by subsequent critics (Cox and Hinchliffe, 1993: 12-13).

 The Waste Land is certainly complicated, though it no longer seems as impenetrable as it did to its first readers. The complexities are at least of four kinds: its disjunctive and discontinuous form, its quotations in foreign languages (Latin, German, French, Italian, and Sanskrit), its various allusions, and its mythic structure. It is Eliot's allusions that will probably cause the most problems for the average reader; references to at least thirty-seven works of art, literature, history, and music can be found in the poem. Further, as Eliot's use of explanatory footnotes suggests, these allusions are not always obvious. Whereas, the allusions in *The Love Song* were relatively familiar, but the references in *The Waste Land* are often known by a few people due to its mystery, including not only the central texts of Western literature, like the Bible, Virgil, Ovid, St. Augustine, Dante, Shakespeare, and Spenser but also poems by Baudelaire, Verlaine, and Nerval, as well as, plays by Thomas Middleton, Ben Webster, Thomas Kyd and John Lyle, and operas by Wagner, a book by Hermann Hesse, and Buddha's Fire Sermon. Like Pound's *Cantos*, Eliot's poem is considered as a compendium or archive of Western civilization; a civilization that has fallen down needs to be put back together (Beach Christopher, 2003: 44). David Perkins explains the use of these allusive "fragments" in the poem:

The individual mind and the civilization are on the edge of a crack-up. Yet the panoramic range and inclusiveness of the poem, which only Eliot's fragmentary and elliptical juxtapositions could have achieved so powerfully in a brief work, held in one vision not only contemporary London and Europe but also human life stretching far back into time. The condition of man seen in the poem was felt to be contemporaneous and perennial, modern yet essentially the same in all times and places (Perkins, 1980: 514).

Kaplan says that the poem, by 1940s, had become a standard in most anthologies of modern poetry: "The poem is so well-known that its name has become a tag for Eliot and for the group of poets who have followed him. This group is commonly known as the 'Waste Land Group'" (Kaplan, 1997: 24-25). It was, as Lawrence Rainey's research into the publication of the poem has shown, famous even before it appeared in 1922, and it has continued to be the most prominent, though not by any means the most popular poem of the twentieth century. In spite of the tremendous cultural authority of the poem that has increased in number over the years and in spite of the fact that it helped to shape a completely new academic discipline devoted to elucidating complex literary works, *The Waste Land* has remained difficult to read. Kaplan points out the factors behind its difficulty, which are the numerous interpretations on the narrative level and because of the piled up contrasts. The poem may be read on a narrative level, which is a story covering a twelve-hour period in a single day. North Michael, argues,

> Some of that difficulty is so intrinsic to the poem that it can never be dispelled, and much contemporary criticism has turned from the new critical effort to explain it in away and has attempted instead to account for its ineradicable mystery (Michael, 2001: IX).

Fear gives the mood of the poem its center of gravity. Fear is everywhere, both in the said and in the unsaid about the modern world. Moreover, it is also in those "filaments" of feeling and experience that cannot be said, because there is no language that can express them.

One can recognize fear also in the poem's voices, and fear gathers like dead leaves in a windy corner along the white spaces when the voices fail. It is part of adolescent experience "And when we were children / . . . I was frightened. He said, Marie, / Marie, hold on tight. And down we went" (ll. 13-16), and she is the companion of the miserable subject in adulthood "Fear death by water. / I see crowds of people, walking round in a ring" (ll. 55-56). Modern men grow so familiar with fear and trembling that they hardly notice how it shapes and accents everything they feel, think, and do. It is the very air that they breathe, and like the dry, dusty desert, it chokes them. Fear is the shadow, which rises to meet them at evening (l. 29). It forces them into the arms of charlatans (a person who considers himself expert especially in medicine) like Madame Sosostris, the fortune-teller, who is the contemporary counterfeit of the prophetic desert voices (ll. 108-110). It is fear that destroys the nerves of the middle-class wife, and also leads her to the dreadful wait for the monstrous revelation, death's "knock upon the door" (l. 138). Fear pays no attention to wealth or class or education; it devastates the aristocrat's stately home and penetrates the working-class pub, with adultery and pain (Cooper, 2006: 70).

The title of the poem comes from Miss Weston's book, *From Ritual to Romance*. Eliot begins with an allusion to her argument that the tradition of the quest for the Holy Grail is rooted in ancient vegetation and fertility myths. Weston relates how the Fisher King has been made impotent by the gods; his kingdom laid to barren waste. In some versions of the legend, she reminds readers that this occurs because of an act of sexual violence the King has committed. The Fisher King awaits a knight who can begin the quest to restore his virility and release his kingdom from his barren state. The theme of the poem is anthropological and the nature of fertility is ritual (Miller, 2006: 132). The anthropological background plays "an obvious part in evoking that particular sense of the unity of life which is essential to the poem", which is "a peculiarly significant expression of the scientific spirit" (Leavis, 1961: 93-94). Leavis in his analysis of 'The Burial of the Dead" demonstrates that the structure of the poem is obvious without the aid of notes, but he admits that the poem is only available for a limited audience although it is the symptom of the culture that produced the poem. Leavis believes that *The Waste Land* is a depiction of the breakdown of traditional modern society:

> In considering our present plight we have also to take account
> of the incessant rapid change that characterizes the Machine
> Age. The result is breach of continuity and the uprooting of
> life. This last metaphor has a peculiar aptness, for what we are
> witnessing today is the final uprooting of the immortal ways of
> life, rooted in the soil (Leavis, 1961: 91).

The Waste Land is also a collection of flash backs, but there is no effect of heterogeneity, since all the flash backs are relevant to the same thing, which together give what seems to be a complete expression of the poet's vision of modern life. The mystery of the modern life can be seen in different ways which no other modern poet has been more successful than Eliot to reveal so adequately the inextricable tangle of the sordid and the beauty that makes up life. First, life is not hellish and second heavenly; it has a purgatorial quality for Eliot, which denotes that deliverance is possible (North, 2001: 137).

Harold Bloom points out that *The Waste Land* can be read as modern Europe mythologized or allegorized; a dead land struck by spiritual famine and drought, where the Fisher King waits for a period of fertility (Bloom, 1999: 41), whereas, one of Eliot's friends, Mary Hutchinson, who read *The Waste Land* after its completion, commented that it was Tom's autobiography. Eliot himself said:

> Various critics have done me the honour to interpret the
> poem in terms of criticism of the contemporary world, have
> considered it, indeed, as an important bit of social criticism. It
> was only the relief of a personal and wholly insignificant grouse
> against life (Valerie Eliot, 1971: 1).

Eliot justified the necessity of autobiography as opposed to formal biography. He believes that there are some definitive experiences of life, which are so private that only the man himself can record. To know the man, one must follow the poem, that alone "will give the pattern of the personal emotion, the personal drama and struggle, which no biography, however, full and intimate, could give us but our experience of the plays themselves" (Eliot's Selected Essays, 1918-1932: 180). Gordon says that Eliot has also pointed out that every poem is "an epitaph", which suggests that the poem is the last word in the life of its author (Gordon, 1977: 86).

The epigraph is translated as, "For I once saw with my own eyes the Cumean Sibyl hanging in a jar, and when the boys asked her: 'Sibyl, what do you want?' She answered 'I want to die'" (Norton Critical, 3rd Edition).

The epigraph resonates with the many voices in the poem that capture the overwhelming question regret of their hollow lives. Sibyl represents the state of world-weariness that the poem explores and criticizes (Miller, 2006: 132).

In the ancient myth, Sibyl had asked the gods for the gift of everlasting life, but forgot to ask for everlasting youth. Thus, she shrivelled with age to a size and delicacy that required her to be kept in a bottle, lest she disintegrates. Her statement speaks of her weariness with life and her desire to be released from it, though she is forced to live forever as the result of her own request. In this way, she is like one of the speakers in the poem who regrets,

"The awful daring of a moment's surrender
Which an age of Prudence can never retract" (Lines, 403-404)

There were about ten Sibyls in the ancient world, prophetesses whom the ancient people, the Greeks and Romans consulted about the future, but the most famous Sibyl is from Cumae, whose mysterious cavern was rediscovered in 1934 by archaeologists of ancient Cumae near Naples. Her prophesies were delivered verses inscribed on palm leaves and placed at the mouth of her cave. One of these collections was put of a charge of a special priestly faculty in Rome, preserved in the underground chambers beneath the temple of Jove on the Capitoline Hill. After this was destroyed in 83 B.C. when the temple burnt down, a new collection was made to replace it. The Cumaean Sibyl, which was in Virgil's Fourth Eclogue, prophesizes and the Christians took it as a foreshadowing for the birth of Christ. Eliot, in the prepublication version of *The Waste Land*, has taken an epigraph from Joseph Conrad's *Heart of Darkness* (1900), as the narrator recounts the death of Kurtz:

> Did he live his life again in every detail of desire, temptation, and surrender during that supreme moment of complete knowledge? He cried in a whisper at some image, at some vision—he cried out twice, a cry that was no more than breath—'The horror! The horror! (Heart of Darkness, 2008: 117).

The Waste Land goes back to Eliot's fantasies of religious extreme in 1914. When Eliot was at the age of twenty-eight, he was living in the Ash Street attic in Cambridge, Massachusetts; at that time he wrote three visionary fragments from which he later took some lines, the setting and idea for part V of *The Waste Land*. The three fragments were concerning revelation and its aftermath: the attractions and problems of "turning" or conversion. The poem shows the difficulty of living of a man who suffers in the two worlds. This for Eliot was no sudden blinding certainty, but a long period of doubt (Gordon, 1977: 87).

The poem begins as a personal means of pulling together one's fragmented consciousness, but in doing so, Eliot manages to present a solution to a world of selfishness by realizing the problems of modern man and finding solutions for them. Through a careful study of the landscapes and urban scenes, Eliot presents the progress of his characters' fates over the course of five sections. A close study of these individuals populating *The Waste Land* further enlightens the search for answers to the drought. Finally, Eliot's rich language will be its own ambiguous key to enlightenment, demanding that the reader can critically consider the scenarios he presents (Batra, 2001: 58).

The poem portrayed the moral, spiritual and economic wasteland of Europe after World War I. Critics are of the viewpoint that this poem launched modern poetry: "Eliot's style in *The Waste Land* is profoundly allusive, echoing so many sources from such diverse historical and geographical contexts that scholars have been busy tracing these allusions since its publication". Moreover, the poem does not only have a single narrative point of view, but, it is composed of many voices, some of them are more central to the trajectory of meaning, others are more peripheral. Eliot's *The Waste Land*, which is, according to F. R. Leavis, a "great and positive achievement and one of the first importance for English poetry," presents the best depiction of modern man's life. Modern people's problems, especially after the First World War, have become extremely difficult to understand. As the natural world has become barren because of the massive death and destruction, the internal state of modern man has also become complex as well as perverted. They experienced a life-in-death situation, always expecting death like "a handful of dust" ("Burial of the Dead"). The moral values were lost, changed and perverted sex has become a part of their daily lives. In fact, innocence is considered as perversion. Like Prufrock, every modern human is hopeless. In this wasteland, the modern men are like the "heap of broken images" where "the dead tree gives no shelter, cricket no relief" ("Burial of the Dead"). Modern Men have lost the true feeling for others that is why sex is loveless. The typist girl, after making love like a machine, feels "glad" when the job is "over" ("The Fire Sermon"). Women have to remain always cautious to prevent their partners from going away to other women. They are merely used as tools for producing children; the overt taking of contraceptives destroy their health, yet, they cannot bear giving birth anymore, so they need pills, but, then, their husbands do not tolerate having such ugly and unproductive wives. Such is the condition of a conjugal life in the modern age. The husband and wife are not loyal to each other, moreover, their relationship is very superficial and they only care about the outer beauty and they neglect all the other kinds of beauty as it is seen in the case of Lil and Albert (Lil's husband):

> "To get yourself some teeth. He did, I was there.
> You have them all out, Lil, and get a nice set,
> He said, I swear, I can't bear to look at you"
> (Lines, 144-146)

Besides, homosexuality has become a terrible threat to moral values. In "the Fire sermon," one sees the Smyrna merchant going through such relationship. Faith in God is overshadowed by the power of money and personal enjoyment. Men, busy with their own business purposes, are crossing the London Bridge at 9 a.m., which is the time of Christ's crucifixion, indicating they are forgetting religious dogmas and are more concerned with their worldly affairs. It is often not easy to understand whose point of view directs certain sections of the poem; yet there is much to be gained from a careful reading of this poem, even without a scholar's background in all the texts and occasions to which it alludes (Miller, 2006:131-132).

Eliot begins part I, of *The Waste Land* like a prophetic voice, which sullenly confronts the spring's snow melting; it also alludes to the burial ceremonies of the Anglican Church and makes the subject of death, and all other metaphors, at the centre of the poem. This part of the poem introduces the themes of a dead world and the need for a search to restore that world to balance. The very beginning of the poem starts with the description of the month of April as the "cruellest" month because it brings death to life; it forces people to survey a horrible blighted land rather than the rebirth modern men wanted. The speaker says: "April is the cruellest month, breeding" (Line, 1). Then, Eliot writes that April breeds "Lilacs out of the dead land, mixing / Memory and desire" (Lines, 2-3). Here the "lilacs" recall Walt Whitman's "When Lilacs Last in the Dooryard Bloomed," written upon the loss of Abraham Lincoln. The lilacs become a reminder of loss, a living thing that recalls death and melancholy. The flowers do not bring joy, but instead make Whitman "mourn with ever-returning spring" (Line, 3). They also make the modern man feel sad. Springtime is just a harbinger of loss. In this cycle, there is no rebirth of life in the spring until the dead of winter have been buried. In fact, winter served to keep the land dead, ironically, by keeping the dead half-alive. Eliot's speaker relates:

> "Winter kept us warm, covering
> Earth in forgetful snow, feeding
> A little life with dried tubers" (Lines, 5-7).

Snow accumulates and makes the mind ignore reality, numbing the world. The narrator relates a subtle desire within him to resist the life-giving spring, and remains undisturbed under the cover of a snowy memory of how things have always been (Spanos, 1979: 245). Memory will prove critical to Eliot in the framework of his epic; it is the means through which he can find his way through the wastes of his world, without it, there is no context; forgetting what has happened before dooms people to know nothing of the future (Ahearn, 2008: 13).

April symbolizes a stage of limbo. It is neither living nor dead. The speaker is talking about the first meeting she had with her disloyal lover:

> "Summer surprised us, coming over the Starnbergersee
> With a shower of rain; we stopped in the colonnade,
> And went on in sunlight, into the Hofgarten,
> And drank coffee, and talked for an hour." She then said:
> "Bin gar keine Russin, stamm' aus Litauen, echt deutsch."
> (Lines, 8-12)

The last line of this stanza means "I'm not Russian, I'm German." This stanza then ends with her telling him her childhood stories as a kind of escape from the modern world because of the failure of the modern man in communication and because of the results of the devastations caused by World War I, and also to highlight that the past image of their childhood that is very innocent (Ahearn, 2008: 14), as seen in the following lines:

> "And when we were children, staying at the archduke's,
> My cousin's, he took me out on a sled,
> And I was frightened, He said, Marie." (Lines, 13-15)

Eliot uses Lilac's colour to symbolize death and the image "tube" (flower bulbs) to indicate the world climate, a stage of inferno, which is also depicted by the April season. The first stanza of the poem contains a few romantic and beautiful imagery from the past, which will not reappear again in the rest of the poem (Keppen, etal, 2000: 256). These degenerating, destructive, decomposing and weakening pastoral imageries serve as a sharp contrast to the horrifying images depicted throughout the rest of the poem, which results in a very disturbing picture of the wasteland, the world which modern men live in.

"The Burial of the Dead," refers to the sacred rite of the Anglican Church by the same name. Dead decaying bodies are buried to take sterility away to the land and to ease their influence on other peoples' minds. Burial is a physical means of showing that the dead are away, which has carried a symbolic significance through its connections to Christ and rebirth. The first section of *The Waste Land* is concerned with the relationship of the earth to its inhabitants, following the ancient Greek element of "earth" and its effects on preserving and destroying, by both giving life and burying it. Normally, dead bodies fertilize the ground so that lilacs can spring up, bringing life out of death. But here in the wasteland, there has been no such burial and renewal; the people exist as the living-dead (Ahearn, 2008: 6).

In *The Waste Land*, Eliot was preoccupied to some degree by the problem of the imprisoned psyche. The poem depicts the image of a momentous crisis of values in Western culture, following the spiritual upheaval of the First World War. Like *The Love Song*, it is a cry for awareness of self-alienation from others and the consequent sense of meaningless characteristic of the modern world. It has often been suggested that the protagonist in *The Waste Land* is identical to the Fisher King which is borrowed from ancient North European myth. A first-person narrator who once speaks of "fishing in the dull canal" (Eliot's Complete Poems and Plays, 1909-1962: 67) says later:

> "I sat upon a shore
> Fishing, with the arid plain behind me
> Shall I at least set my lands in order?" (Lines, 423-425)

It can be said that this speaker can be considered as a modern Fisher King, and to consider him as a single personality is disrupted in this context by the lament of Prince Ferdinand for his father's death, which is borrowed from William Shakespeare's *The Tempest*. After this speaker's fishing scene in the dull canal Tiresias could clearly stand for the image of modern man:

> "I Tiresias though blind, throbbing between two lives,
> Old man with wrinkles of female breasts, can see
> At the violet hour, the evening hour that strives
> Homeward, and brings the sailor home from the sea,
> The typist home at teatime clears her breakfast, lights
> Her stove, and lays out food in tins" (Lines, 418-423)

The Fisher King, like Tiresias in this passage, speaks in the first person so that his distinct identity seems unmistakable, but his voice and vision are juxtaposed sharply, as in a collage. This structural method, which is familiar to all readers of *The Waste Land*, typifies the arrangement of the poem as a whole. Though Tiresias is not a character in the poem, he could unify the other characters in the poem, for example, the one-eyed merchant "melts into" the Phoenician sailor, who in turn is not wholly distinct from Ferdinand, Prince of Naples. Moreover, "all women are one woman, the two sexes meet in Tiresias" (Eliot's Complete Poems and Plays, 1909-1962: 78).

After the loveless scene between the typist and the insensitive young friend, Tiresias reveals his presence and says:

> "And I Tiresias have foresuffered all
> Enacted on this same divan and bed;
> I who sat by Thebes blew the wall
> And walked among the lowest of the dead"
> (Lines, 243-246)

The love-making scene illustrates the failure between the physically alienated modern men of the modern wasteland that is very similar to the scene in the second section, which depicts the elegant woman and her husband as a sample of the modern man's inability to break down barriers genuinely shared feeling between them (J. Scott, 1991: 42).

> "What are you thinking of? What thinking? What?
> I never know what you are thinking. Think"
> (Lines, 113-114)

The woman protests and shows the fragile condition of an alienated ego, while the husband's reply suggests the mental inertia of one who is unable to leave the bondage of listless self-absorption:

> "I think we are in rats' alley
> Where the dead men lost their bones" (Lines, 115-116)

The Waste Land centers around death and resurrection, revealing the connection between sensuality and anxiety, between sin and sensuality. The poem, because of some inexplicable insufficiency in human nature, delineates the modern man as liable to the sexual temptations lead to suffering and death; man's history is nothing but "birth, copulation, and death." Sin, lust, evil, and death form a circle among which there is the mutual cause and effect relation. Therefore, earthly love, even in its most intense form, as seen between the lover and the hyacinth girl, with its romantic associations, will fail man in the end (George, 1969: 152).

The conception of death is the substance of *The Waste Land*. Frazer's *The Golden Bough* and Jessie Weston's book, *From Ritual to Romance*, provide the basic framework of resurrection, where many allusions to classical and mythological quotations, images, and symbols are used to remind the modern man of what has happened to the previous peoples of different countries, which suggests the theme of death and the need of redemption.

Sibyl's request for death at the beginning of the poem implies her dislike of an everlasting life. After the request, Marie's memory makes people associate her life with the death of her three cousins in the war. Unnatural death suggests the miserable condition of life, like death of many people during the war. Words suggesting the meaning of death occur 25 times in the poem. By demonstrating the dirty love of several women, Eliot suggested the indifference between man and woman. Moreover, women's being either the object or the subject of sensuality implies the misfortune of women in a male chauvinist world. It can be said that the poem has not concluded with restoration of health but with the recurrence of mortal illness. (Blistein, 2008: 10).

Two other major themes can be detected in *The Waste Land*, which mirror the psychic and mental state of the modern man. The first one is disillusionment, which reflects the current state of affairs in modern society, especially the post-World War I Europe in which Eliot lived. The sense of disillusionment is illustrated in several ways; the most prominent of which are references to fertility rituals and joyless sex. First Eliot draws on the types of fertility legends discussed in Weston's and Frazer's books, for example, in the beginning of the first section, the poet uses an extended image of a decomposing corpse lying underground in winter, which "kept us warm, covering / Earth in forgetful snow, feeding / a little life with dried tubers." A tuber is the fleshy part of an underground stem, but here it stands for modern man's flesh feeding new plants. Human society is so disappointed that it has undergone a moral death, an idea on which Eliot plays throughout the poem (Keppen, etal, 2000: 256). In fact, Eliot raises a new idea, "a little life." in the second stanza, which opposes the theme of death suggested in the first stanza however, the land is all "stony rubbish," where roots and branches do not grow, and "the dead tree gives no shelter," and there is "no sound of water." Eliot also expresses disillusionment through the events of the unhappy sex, such as the case of Philomel, upon whom sex is forced. In fact, Eliot employs a litany of joyless sexual situations, including the rich couple who would rather play chess than have sex, and the poor couple for whom sex becomes a way only of pleasing the husband, and even then, only if the wife has "a nice set" of teeth. There is no love in any of these unions, and in the case of the poor couple, the wife has started having abortions because she "nearly died of young George," one of her children. This purposeful killing of a new life is another way Eliot shows how people are disillusioned regarding sex and how procreative power in many cases is lost. But perhaps the most prominent example of meaningless sex comes during the scene between the typist and the clerk. Following this joyless sexual encounter, in which the man satisfies his lust, he leaves the woman, who is "Hardly aware of her departed lover." Her indifference shows in her simple actions that "She smoothes her hair with automatic hand, / And puts a record on the gramophone (Lines, 255-256). Her hand, like the sex itself, is "automatic," without emotion.

Restoration is considered the second major theme, which contrasts disillusionment. If modern society can overcome its disillusionment, it will be restored back to a condition in which life once again has meaning and all people can coexist together. Eliot in his poem presents an example that is the Fisher King Myth taken from Weston's book, and compares the modern life with the past events. Yet throughout the poem, when one refers to this idea, it is generally handled in more subtle ways than the references that underline the idea of disillusionment and hopelessness. For instance, in the first section, "the hyacinth girl" says:

> "You gave me hyacinths first a year ago;
> They called me the hyacinth girl.'
> -Yet when we came back, late, from the hyacinth garden,
> Your arms full, and your hair wet, I could not
> Speak, and my eyes failed, I was neither
> Living nor dead, and I knew nothing,
> Looking into the heart of light, the silence"
> (Lines 35-41).

Hyacinths are often associated with the idea of resurrection, which, in the context of this poem, is looked at as the aim of the poet. The above lines also show that modern man tries to do everything for the sake of his pleasure, a pleasure that is void of all kinds of love, respect, and loyalty. But as soon as he introduces the idea, Eliot experiences the inability of modern man to speak and with an image of disillusionment that is pinpointed: "I could not speak, and my eyes failed, / I was neither living nor dead, and I knew nothing." The idea of restoration, in the form of resurrection, is not explored in detail until the final section, with the introduction of Christ. The final section begins with the account of Christ's betrayal and death and of "the shouting and the crying" of Christ's followers of his death. With Christ's death, "We who were living are now dying." Lost without their savior, Christians feel morally dead. But in the distinct forms and rules of traditional poetry, poets often sought uniformity in length and meter of the stanza (Keppen, etal, 2000: 256-257). Those poets, who could work within these challenging rules, and could still express themselves in a unique or an attractive way, were considered good poets. But, particularly after World War I, as literature and other arts shifted from a traditional, romantic, or idealized approach to an approach that emphasized gritty realism full of discontinuity and despair, when artists began to experiment with nontraditional forms, ideas, and styles. Disillusioned by the war, artists and writers such as Eliot rebelled against the logical, traditional thinking, which they believed, helped start and make the war worse. Collectively, as many critics have noted that the staggering modernistic effect of this work sets off a bomb in the public consciousness.

The poem is filled with the sense of distraction, agony, and extreme despair of modern man by comparing the ends of the five parts of *The Waste Land*. The consciousness of death in the poem demonstrates dialectic features. The collection of many broken elements proposes a unified concept: death is revival. In the mind of the poet, death does not belong to the future tense, nor does it exist beyond life, and it does not hide behind the reality. Death exists in the present, and it is depicted as the modern man's process of life. Thereafter modern man lives in anxiety and in the fear of death (Robinson, 2001: 38).

Eliot's stress on city life and the miserable marriage did not make him silent, but gave him more "living material" for his poetry; a gift on full display in "A Game of Chess." This part of *The Waste Land* consists of a two-part exploration of contemporary sexual relationships, the first in a lady's dressing room and the second in a pub. The dressing room scene features characters resembling Eliot and his wife. He invited both his wife and Ezra Pound to comment on the typescript, and both noted the parallel (Gish and Laity, 2004:139).

At the end of the first section, the death of Marcello is not associated with the hope of spiritual redemption and resurrection, for he has not been incorporated into the body of believers. Thus, his burial is not a Christian one, but similar to the primitive burial practices of nature worshippers, without any positive certainty about salvation. Cornelia's words resemble Ophelia's distracted words at the end of the second section. The third section ends with reference to the strength of passion over reason; the fourth ends by referring to death and the fifth ends in madness. The significance of such endings lies in the failure of modern man to achieve spiritual synthesis without faith; and without faith, man is condemned to anxiety, despair, passion, madness, and death (George, 1969: 154).

The Waste Land presents Eliot's attitude to the continuous problems of modern men experiencing, pain, and evil. Eliot's emotions must have been deeply moved by the events of the First World War, which made him speculate upon human destiny. Eliot sees suffering as inseparable from modern man's life. His religious sense makes him ascribe human suffering to human sinfulness. Since human nature is radically sinful, man is subject to pains and suffering at all times. Just as man cannot completely get rid of his sexual appetites, so he cannot completely eradicate evil and suffering. Eliot's consciousness of death lies deeply in the present, but it also anticipates the future resurrection, mixed with his inclination to tradition and religion. Therefore, the poet is both a pessimistic realist and an optimistic romantic. The greatest virtue of *The Waste Land* is that Eliot presents the modern mind and modern city as composed of fragments from the past, "a heap of broken images" through which great and obsessive anxieties run. In regard to Eliot's belief in redemption, the stories of the Golden Bough and of the Fisher King reveal his ideal. In the fifth section, "What the Thunder Said," freedom and holiness, become possible, according to both Dante and Buddha, when passions, lusts, and sins are eliminated, and the duality of fire stems from the fact that it represents both the sin and the method of purgation.

When *The Waste Land* is considered as a modern poem to have a "positive" message, it may lie precisely in the strange negative strategy that aims to rescue modern man from the life-in-death misery, or perhaps only Eliot himself in that moment of desperation, from immorality, personal despair, and a new freedom in a modernity that increasingly seemed meaningless. If the way back from all that meant the acceptance of cruelty blowing "the gaff on human nature" (For

Lancelot Andrewes: Essays, 1928:51), and of a hundred other refusals to compromise the "belief in Divine Grace" (Eliot's Selected Essays, 1932: 17), then all people should have the courage to stare at the truth in the face, and not to make a sudden movement out of fear (Cooper, 2006: 68). *The Waste Land* is seen to define the twentieth century: its employment of different, often conflicting voices; its experiments with chronology, sequence, and structure and its extensive use of allusion, especially to medieval and Renaissance works; the poem's portrayal of a world in which all certainties had been shattered and human beings wandered in a futile search for meaning; their fundamental pessimism about the state of human beings in a world that had seen two unimaginably destructive wars within thirty years of each other; all of these mirror the qualities of the time itself (Milne and Kelly, 2000: 125).

Singh Rajni argues that a world that is devoid of any healthy relationship makes its people mentally fragile. Eliot felt that the moral corruption and the loss of spirituality had resulted in uncertainty, isolation and the desire for death. One of the main features of *The Waste Land* is uncertainty. Modern man has become an isolated being because of the prevailing unhealthy social relationships. Though being in the crowd, he finds himself alone, and because of his sense of isolation, "modern man has no objective in his life, he craves for death" as in the case with Sybil who wishes to die when the children asked her about what does she want. (Singh, 2005: 177).

The Waste Land is a poem, which has begun and rooted within the deep recesses of past memory, and it relies upon these connections to make sense of the present and moves forward without having strong connections among its sections. Thrown into a world of materialism and human isolation and devoid of passion and hope, Eliot seeks a mist in the middle of the drought; a shower of hope to wash the world anew. Recalling the myths of history in recounting the legends and literature of the past, Eliot is not simply discussing a common theme in world literature. He does not write dispassionately from a distance, nor does he sum up a state of affairs that can be prodded with a pen and then forgotten; Eliot wrote in the middle of his own torment, with his world drying up around him. In the midst of some "hysteria," he could not rectify what he wrote, and this poem is the therapeutic result of that period (Koestenbaum, 1988: 115; Gold, 2000: 519-20).

Several desperate voices including an unnamed Prufrock-like speaker, Marie, a Lithuanian German of royal decent, the hyacinth girl, and Madame Sosostris, "famous clairvoyant" helped Eliot to compose this section. These voices speak of Europe where the royal classes had dull and meaningless life, which is suffused with nostalgic memories, where vision and voice are impossible, and where the dead strolls in the living. The stanzas of the first section depict the image and the mood of deep apathy in a dead world occupied by the living dead. Thus, the Prufrock-like persona cannot speak to or see the hyacinth girl with her arms full of flowers (Miller, 2006: 132).

Leonard Unger points out that the theme of the failure of communication, of a positive relationship between a man and a woman is found in his other early poems like *Hysteria* and *La Figlia che Piange*, and it later becomes a major theme of the whole body of Eliot's work, which is one of the most prominent dilemmas of modern man. It appears early in *The Waste Land* with the image of the hyacinth girl (Unger, 1961: 10):

> Yet when we came back, late, from the Hyacinth garden,
> Your arms full, and your hair wet, I could not
> Speak, and my eyes failed, I was neither
> Living nor dead, and I knew nothing,
> Looking into the heart of light, the silence."
> (Lines, 37-41)

The theme of failure of communication is developed by various means throughout Eliot's poetry and plays. It becomes related to other emerging themes, especially to the religious meanings, as seen in the symbolic imagery of the "rose-garden", which appears in *Ash Wednesday, Four Quartets, The Family Reunion,* and *The Confidential Clerk* (Unger, 1961: 10).

Eliot also introduces his readers to the first players in his tragicomedy: the hyacinth girl, Stetson, St. Narcissus, and Madame Sosostris among others. Throughout the poem, the players appear to be essentially incarnations of the same characters, though in different settings and various positions. The women, who were caught between fecundity and creative forces form a central character in the entirety of *The Waste Land,* appear in "The Burial of the Dead" to establish the parameters for the character, a person somewhere between the pragmatic Sosostris and her poisonous "Belladonnas." Marie longs for a past life, and Sosostris relates an uncongenial image of the future. Likewise Eliot's men are similarly impotent, compensating for their lack of sense through an opportunism that leads to further isolation; St. Narcissus finds himself drying out in the desert instead of finding relief in the shadows, and the other men are either forgetful or buried (Diemert Brian, 1988: 175-180).

Probably the most explicit portrayal of the physical wasteland is seen in the first section of the poem "The Burial of the Dead":

> What are the roots that clutch, what branches grow
> Out of this stony rubbish? Son of man,
> You cannot say, or guess, for you know only
> A heap of broken images, where the sun beats,
> And the dead tree gives no shelter, the cricket no relief,
> And the dry stone no sound of water. Only
> There is shadow under this red rock,
> (Come in under the shadow of this red rock),
> And I will show you something different from either
> Your shadow at morning striding behind you
> Or your shadow at evening rising to meet you;
> I will show you fear in a handful of dust"
> (Lines 19-30).

The above lines show that the modern world is a hot dry and stony place in which one can find no relief. The sun, instead of being the source of energy, it only makes the landscape dry further; the trees, which might once have offered shelter from the heat and intensity of the sun, are now dead branches, which can provide no relief. The decay and destruction of human values in the world is evoked in this passage: "images which once gave meaning to our experience have now become meaningless bits and pieces, piled in a refuse heap, a jumble which we call culture" (Lawrence, 1985: 324).

The images of *The Waste Land* are both poetic and cultural. The above lines show that the images are broken poetic images. The speaker's question, "What are the roots that clutch, what branches grow/ Out of this stony rubbish?" asks about two things, first, what sort of meaningful life can grow in this wasteland, and second, what sort of modern poem can be created out of the fragments of the past at the poet's disposal. Some biblical allusions are also found in the poem, the reference to "shadow under the red rock" probably alludes to Isaiah that depicts the righteous king "as rivers in a dry place, as the shadow of a great rock in a weary land," which actually depict a godless and barren world (Lawrence etal, 1985: 324).

The only promise of relief in *The Waste Land* is the speaker's offer of shelter under the red rock; this promise brings a kind of revelation, as it is clear in "I will show you something different." But the hope of revelation is diminished at the end of the above lines, in which modern man's morality is frighteningly revealed in: "I will show you fear in a handful of dust". In *The Waste Land*, the search for salvation can only bring the painful knowledge of man's vulnerability and impotence (Lawrence etal, 1985: 324).

Williamson says that latent in the "dead tree" and the "red rock" and the colour of "The Fire Sermon", is the burial of Christ, which involves the preserver of the Grail and fetches the journey to Emmaus in part V. The speaker, who always echoes the prophetic note, will show modern man some thing different from the shadow of time in *The Waste Land*; he will show him "fear in a handful of dust." Williamson believes that if this image begins with the Biblical association, it will end by the vegetation myths. The garden scene, which is framed by the sailor's melancholic song in Tristan, is translated as:

> "Fresh blows the wind from off the bow,
> My Irish maid, where lingerest thou?" (Lines, 31-32)

It is a story of a tragic passion. The question "where lingerest thou?" is at the end answered by "desolate and empty the sea." It must not be forgotten that the garden scene accounts for the answer. The capitalized Hyacinth suggests the vegetation god and a victim of love. It is observed that the protagonist's response is striking: a failure of speech and sight, a state of neither living nor dead, describing the effect of the vision of the Grail upon the impure modern society. A love-death would be precisely framed by snatches of song from Wagner's *Tristan und Isolde*, but the sea expresses a change. The German makes the reader go back to the scene with Marie and amplifies its associations (Williamson, 1953: 131-132).

Eliot's references to the garden scene in section II is very important. The final meaning of what is to be discovered in "the heart of light, the silence," remains to be answered. As the poet experiences fear; the connections of the fear acquire a new setting in the fortune. For a moment, one may venture this statement: the initial state of the mind is defined by the experience of spring followed by the experience of *The Waste Land*; "the roots that clutch" are those of fear, and their origin is found in the "hyacinth garden" (Williamson, 1953: 132).

Madame Sosostris was introduced in the poem because she is a fortune-teller, but because of her cold, her fortune telling is made uneasy and also her magic made powerless. However, her wisdom is the best in Europe, but she is involving in a malicious pack of cards. Eliot connects Madame Sosostris with the Sailor Tarot card. Her name is interesting for the fact that it embodies two iterations of the Mores Code distress signal "SOS." The—tris suffix appended is a variation of the suffix—trix (also spelled—trice) that is affixed to Latin loanwords to signify a feminine agent corresponding to the masculine agenting suffix—tor. This signifies that Madame Sosostris is an agent specializing in sending the distress call "SOS." Of what distress does she call? The Sailor Tarot card, or, as Eliot says, "the drowned Phoenician Sailor," is Eliot's symbol for death, which has spread from the war fronts to the cities. The floods of people on the London Bridge of "The Unreal City" may also be the spiritual remains of the buried casualties of the war since in the next passage Eliot introduces Stetson of whom he asks if the corpse he had planted in his garden had "begun to sprout?" Madame Sosostris's distress call is for the walking living-dead and walking dead-dead. Juxtapose this with Marie and the statement emerges that freedom can and could only be where there was no war.

The "fortune-telling," which is taken ironically by a twentieth-century audience, becomes true as the poem develops true in a sense in which Madame Sosostris herself does not think it true. The subject of the fortune-telling accounts for the meaning of the rest of the poem. In general, the limitations of this fortune-teller, and the irony of the poem, appear in what she does not see. Her clairvoyance does not become the cause of an identification of the protagonist with Ferdinand, but only with the drowned Phoenician sailor. The line from *The Tempest* which is a suggestion for this identification connects the "pearls that were his eyes" with the preceding experience, "my eyes failed." This is an image of modern man, which in the present context is committed to death. The irony of her defects is more apparent in her failures to see what she mentions. The voice of the irony begins to be heard in this section. In terms of the cards, there is none greater than to "fear death by water." If "dear Mrs. Equitone" is the lady of nerves in the second part, one may add it to the irony. There is no doubt; one must not forget it in the line, "one must be so careful these days" lest this wisdom falls into the wrong hands. But the most significant irony is the restoration of a greater meaning of life by means of "wicked pack of cards." Although he was one of the dead, "I had not thought death had undone so many" and the city appears "unreal" as it does not appear the same to them. They do not share his misgivings about the wasteland, and they are not conscious of the cruelty of April or of "a dead sound on the final stroke of mine" (Luke 23:44). He mixes and mingles his fortune with reality, which is the illusionary aspect of the poem, and assumes Hamlet's mask of irony or madness when the apparent contrast seems very great. Death echoes through this section until it ends in "That corpse you planted last year in your garden." People do not plant corpse except in vegetation ceremonies; and the reader is also reminded of the "hyacinth garden," of the slain hyacinth and the garden experience (Williamson, 1953: 132-134).

Critics have seen fertility as an important theme in *The Waste Land*. In an early review, Edmund Wilson describes Eliot's poem as "a desolate and sterile country, ruled over by an impotent king, in which not only have the corpse stopped to grow and the animals to reproduce their kind, but the very human inhabitants have become unable to bear children" (Wilson, 1922: 611). In *New Bearings in English Poetry* (1932), F. R. Leavis reads the references to "Vegetation cults" and "fertility ritual" as a reminder of the "remoteness" of modern "human culture" from "natural rhythms": "Sex here is sterile, breeding not life and fulfillment but disgust and unanswerable questions" (Leavis, 1932: 90-93). Cleanth Brooks refers to infertility as a symbol of the decline of Christianity's influence: for Eliot "Christian terminology is a mass of cliché" since he cannot deal with the Christian subject directly, "the theme of resurrection is made on the surface in terms of the fertility rituals" (Brooks, 1968: 86). Similarly, Northrop Frye suggests that inhabitants of the wasteland:

> live the "buried life" of seeds in winter: they wait for the
> spring rains resentfully, for real life would be their death . . .
> Physical death is the final judgment between the seeds who can
> understand the commands of the thunder and die to new life,
> and those who merely die and are rejected, as the sterile seed is
> rejected by nature (Frye, 1963: 64-65).

Stephen Spender ends the focus upon infertility, the essence of Eliot's "method" of contacting public and private spheres. The key idea is that the private failure of the sacrifice and sacrament, which is a ritual between bride and bridegroom, is the result of the public failure of creativity within the civilization. Recent critics continue focusing upon the question of fertility. James E. Miller says that Eliot himself is "the fisher-king suffering the sexual wound (loss of Verdenal) that has rendered him impotent in his marriage like the fisher-king of the wasteland legend." (Miller, 2006: 73). Sandra Gilbert and Susan Gubar read Eliot's "mysteriously sterile Fisher King" as an instance of the modern man emasculated by the war's dehumanization of the soldiers, on the one hand, and its empowerment of women in various ways, on the other: "the gloomily bruised modernist antiheroes churned out by the war suffer specifically from sexual wounds, as if all have become not just no-men, nobodies, but not men, unmen" (Gilbert and Gubar, 1988: 260). Even in Harriet Davidson's reading of the poem as an expression of a hermeneutic philosophy, fertility figures prominently as a symbol of meaningful being-in-the-world: "By the end of the poem, the spring rain will undergo an interpretive metamorphosis from a cruel to a saving release, as generation and interpretation are chosen over sterility and rigidity" (Davidson Harriet, 1985: 99).

The community's sexual and spiritual impotence and degradation are conveyed in almost every section of the poem; one speaker's inarticulate encounter with the hyacinth girl and Lil's abortion to save her degrading marriage, and the young man's indifferent sexual conquest of the typist, like the physical barrenness of the landscape, function as symptoms of the spiritual impotence of the community, a relationship represented by the multiple myths alluded to in the poem.

The central condition of drought and the situation of waiting for rain, which consists of the various myths, become the dominant condition in the poem, in which "rain" is that nourishment which will revive a dying culture in body and spirit (Lawrence, 1985: 323).

Neil Roberts, in his book, *A Companion to Twentieth-Century Poetry*, indicates that John Haffenden has pointed out that "What the Thunder Said", is depicting the image of the present decaying of Eastern Europe, denoting that certain passages of *The Waste Land* were indeed meant to express a "mode of criticism of the contemporary world" (Roberts, 2003: 382).

Weston has pointed out that the figure of the king in *The Waste Land* is wounded rather than dead though the dead or wasteland in the Grail legend results from a possibly deadly infirmity of the king. The corpse and the wound are central images in making the concept of hopelessness a way of understanding the poem's moods and the behavior of its characters (Weston Jessie's From Ritual to Romance, 1957).

Weston's aim was partly to focus on the wealth of narrative materials related to this important theme in the European culture, and partly mystical. Her work belongs to a widespread interest at the time in the magic and the wise literature on which it was based. Weston further argued that what began as pagan fertility rituals in ancient Greece and the Near East, evolved over centuries into the narrative romances that tell of the quest for the Grail, tales such as Wolfram van Eschenbach's Parzival cycle or Geoffrey of Monmouth's Prophetia Merlini in England, which belong to the twelfth century. Eliot's intent in this movement from ritual practices to narrative legends is, in a sense, to put the process in reverse; that is, to find within the legendary materials, that have come to the reader as fiction, their original basis in religious ritual; in other words, to reconstitute their most ancient core. The aim, in the contemporary setting, is to make "an inactive and stagnant society and culture. In post-First World War Europe, it was not the occult to assert that European civilization and values were at a very low ebb" (Cooper, 2006: 64).

Cooper says that *The Waste Land* is a text of the First World War and its aftermath, which does not only reflect the spirit of the times, but it is also a very personal document. When the First World War ended, Eliot's financial and domestic situations had not changed.

Worries over money, his wife's abdominal and gynecological disorders, her increasingly fragile mental state, and his own feelings of nervous exhaustion fed a growing sense of despair. The immediate postwar situation in Britain and Europe added to the sense of collapse and chaos. The disorder in Europe was particularly upsetting. He was aware of the situation in Central and Eastern Europe through his work for Lloyds (Cooper, 2006: 63).

The din of the corrupted inwardness of the modern world is what one reads in a great many parts of *The Waste Land*. Madame Sosostris, the house agent's clerk, the typist and Sweeney, all express the same "eternal message," which highlights the image of modern man. The exhausted despair of the Thames-daughters at the end of "The Fire Sermon" allows the reader to hear the nihilism of the culminating word, "Nothing" (l. 305); the result of what for Eliot amounted to the swindle of Whig-liberal rhetoric. In the song of the Thames-daughters (ll. 266-306), two literary references stand out; Eliot himself draws attention to Richard Wagner's Gotterdammerung in his notes to the passage (Eliot's Collected Poems, 1968: 83), and the reference to the Elizabethan court with the Queen and her lover, the Earl of Leicester, sailing the Thames during her reign in the late sixteenth century. The religious resonance of the phrase "humble people," like the allusions to Wagner and Elizabeth, functions as a sardonic diminution of the three singers and of the valueless inwardness that they express. The Thames-daughters are unable to position present experience in a wider, external context that transforms inwardness into something more vital and significant. The carefully chosen literary and religious allusions contrast with the so-called "lyricism" of "the inner voice." The salvation of the modern man, it seems, does not mean knowing oneself better, but incorporating into a culture of custom and ceremony whose rooted orderliness and organic emotional life make sense of the inner chaos (Cooper, 2006: 67).

The title of section I, "The Burial of the Dead," is a phrase from the Anglican burial service that refers to the dead people and dead land of World War I as well as to the dead body of the Fisher King, and thus, symbolically, to the death of civilization itself. It begins with some of the most celebrated lines in all of modern poetry:

"April is the cruelest month, breeding
Lilacs out of the dead land, mixing
Memory and desire, stirring
Dull roots with spring rain.
Winter kept us warm, covering
Earth in forgetful show, feeding
A little life with dried tubers" (Lines, 1-7).

The first line clearly echoes the opening of another famous long poem, Chaucer's *Canterbury Tales*: "Whan that Aprille with his shoures soote / The droughte of March hath perced to the roote." Yet it is an ironic echo: where Chaucer's prologue celebrates the renewing and engendering powers of spring, Eliot's speaker points to the memories that are not solved and desires the season brings to the surface. The two statements are based on paradox: while April is "the cruellest month," it is winter that "kept us warm." For the speaker, it is winter snow and not spring rain that proves comforting, sustaining the speaker's "little life" without forcing the painful encounter with the past that the rest of the poem represents. The speaker, who could be called the poem's first protagonist, is an inhabitant of the wasteland; he is also the poet, who identifies himself through his perfect control of poetic language. The language here is highly lyrical in a poem where lyricism is not the dominant mode, as if it is written to demonstrate the possibility of a traditional lyric mode in the twentieth century (Beach, 2003: 45-46)

The changes of desire and memory are the thematic threads that hold the poem together. Desires are of different kinds: the desire for death expressed by the Cumaean Sibyl, the sexual desire of the house agent's clerk for the young typist, the brutal desire that causes King Tereus to rape Philomel, and Philomel's desire at the end of the poem to sing like the swallow. Desire is depicted as a dangerous commodity: it can lead to disappointment, to frustration, to sordid affairs and unwanted children, and even to violence. The protagonist distrusts desire, preferring winter's dullness and forgetfulness to the "stirring," "mixing," and "breeding" of spring. Memory also takes various forms in the poem: there is the cultural memory of which the poem's many allusions are the emblems, the mythic memory of vegetation rituals and sacred quests, the historical memory of the war and the decay of Europe, the personal memories of Eliot (his unhappy marriage, mental breakdown, and recovery), and the memories of various characters including Marie and the "hyacinth girl" in "The Burial of the Dead." For Marie memory is her engagement in Alpine sledding. Most significantly, Marie says that when in the mountains, presumably sledding, one feels free. This is important on two levels. Sledding is a pursuit of leisure for some and for others a competitive sport that in either case gives enjoyment and health, and it is a worthwhile pursuit that gives meaning to life. This idea relates strongly to Eliot's ultimate message in *The Waste Land*; that of mourning the devastation of earth, the death of the surface of earth and earth's fruit of life spanning from vegetation to human, by the ravaging war. Bolton and School say that the modern man might leave the city and find solace and solitude in the natural world, like the English romantic poets who left the urban life and joined the natural world especially mountains (Bolton and School, 2009: 200). The mountains especially the Alpine mountains, a strong symbol for always-neutral Switzerland were not part of the war fronts and therefore, were not devastated and wasted (Beach, 2003: 46). Yet Bolton and School argue that perhaps, a return to the primitive life and especially nature can free modern man from his sense of alienation that they are spiritually at distance from other people while they are physically close to. But when one reaches the mountains in the fifth section of the poem, there is neither communion nor solitude. They are dry, lifeless, and as wasted as the city:

> "There is not even silence in the mountains
> But dry sterile thunder without rain
> There is not even solitude in the mountains
> But red sullen faces sneer and snarl
> From doors of mudcracked houses" (Lines, 41-45).

Even the mountains do not offer a sort of rest for the modern urban people and the mountains seem like a nightmarish version of the city, "a phantasmagoric landscape where the elements of the earlier sections of the poem recombine in strange and disturbing ways" (Bolton and School, 2009: 200).

It is perhaps the figure of the blind seer Tiresias, whom Eliot identifies in the footnotes as "the most important personage in the poem who unites all the rest," who best encompasses both memory and desire.

As the poem's "spectator," Tiresias is fated to remember all the scenes he witnesses during his long life, "And I Tiresias have foresuffered all / Enacted on this same divan or bed." As an androgynous (unclear sex) figure, that has experienced being both a man and a woman "throbbing between two lives, / Old man with wrinkled female breasts," he has a double acquaintance with desire. In one version of the Tiresias myth, he was blinded by Hera for saying that women enjoy sex more than men, yet the opposite is the case in the scene he witnesses between the typist and the office clerk in "The Fire Sermon". Here, the young man is clearly the aggressor in the sexual act, and the uncaring woman lets herself be seduced more out of boredom and exhaustion than out of any interest in her lover. Eliot considers this encounter clearly emblematic of the modern wasteland as it influences the lives of both men and women. The pompousness and insensitivity of the clerk "One of the low on whom assurance sits / As a silk hat on a Bradford millionaire", the boring routine, and tawdry existence of the woman, and the utter sterility of their relationship all point to a fallen modern world. Eliot ends the passage with an ironic commentary:

"When lovely woman stoops to folly and
Paces about her room again, alone,
She smoothes her hair with automatic hand,
And puts a record on the gramophone" (Lines, 53-56).

The "automatic hand" here is a synecdoche for the generally automatized life of the woman: she works as a typist, which is itself a monotonous form of labour, and her movements of pacing the room, smoothing her hair, and putting a record on the record player suggest that she is caught in a groove from which she cannot escape. The typist can be compared with the other modern women who populate the poem, like Lil, a drained mother of five with decaying teeth, and the hysterical middle-class wife who declares to her husband, "My nerves are bad tonight. Yes, bad. Stay with me." The lines also contain an allusion to Oliver Goldsmith's eighteenth-century novel *The Vicar of Wakefield*, in which the seduced and deserted Olivia sings that when "lovely woman stoops to folly," the only solution for her shame and grief is to die.

The modern woman in Eliot's poem is not a romantic heroine but a naturalistic inhabitant of the urban metropolis who has no intention of dying: instead, her complete emotional detachment from her own situation represents a kind of death-in-life. If scenes of modern urban life dominate the first four sections of the poem, the final section, "What the Thunder Said," moves outside the city to a desert landscape, where "there is no water but only rock." Here the vision of London as an "Unreal City" expands to include the destruction of various civilizations: "Jerusalem Athens Alexandria / Vienna London / Unreal." The wandering protagonist finally reaches a chapel in the mountains. With the quest nearly at an end, the rain comes and landscapes shift again, this time arriving at the shores of the Indian Ganges, which is a more spiritual counterpart to London's Thames. The sound of the thunder is imagined as a heavenly voice, which speaks the syllable "DA," the source of the three great disciplines of Hindu thought: "data" (give), "dayadhvam" (sympathize), "damyata" (control). To give, in the sense of surrendering oneself to another, is the direct opposite of desire; it is an act that needs an "awful daring" in an "age of prudence." Sympathy or compassion for others will allow people to leave the "prison" of our own consciousness that has in part created *The Waste Land*. Finally, the control of man's baser natures will allow him to achieve a kind of effortless harmony with the divine force. The new awareness that comes with these disciplines provides a means by which the protagonist, now figured explicitly as the Fisher King, can at last "set lands in order." The poem ends with an explosion of fragments in different languages, which indicates a change in modern man's way of perceiving life and offering a variety and mixture of vision of a fallen bridge, a ruined tower, and a refining fire. This destroying and abolishing moment is in turn followed by the thrice-repeated Sanskrit word shantih, "the peace which surpasseth understanding" with which the poem ends. An ending in which scraps of Western literature mix with the ancient wisdom of the Upanishads (any of a class of the Sanskrit sacred books which probably composed between 400 and 200 B.C. embodying the mystical doctrines of ancient Hindu philosophy), is by any standard highly uncertain and it must have appeared almost so complicated and difficult to most of Eliot's first readers, yet it is an appropriate conclusion to such a fundamentally unstable poem. The ending of *The Waste Land* was at this stage of his life, the closest Eliot could come to anything resembling formal or thematic closure. Eliot's readers would have to wait twenty more years, until the completion of *The Four Quartets*, for an ending that affirmed an unambiguous spiritual doctrine (Beach, 2003: 48).

The Waste Land, like the *Divine Comedy*, is another *Pilgrim's Progress* through hell and towards heaven. By recounting one can see locations and hear individuals that might have come directly from Dante's poem, a progression can be identified that has taken place. In the "Burial of the Dead" readers entered hell's entrance, saw the souls of those men who had sought meaning in the wrong place like St. Narcissus, Marie's companion and Stetson, who had no loyal, faithful and dependable fellow but to themselves. "A Game of Chess" took readers deeper within the hell. It shows readers the hollow pleasures of wealth, which is regarded as a source of evil and corruption and the victimization of women, like the woman in the chamber, Lil and the friends in the bar. Misbegotten relationships had given birth to loneliness, isolation, and destruction of modern man. People are seen frozen in their hopeless modern world like those trapped in Dante's *Icy Cocytus* for having betrayed others and themselves (Inferno, XXXXI-IV).

After the decaying of modern world, it is obvious that the old man was drowned in "Death by Water" and it is thought that the world is ritually cleansed through this baptism. This purgation of malice had a marked effect of drowning sexual and false desires. With the drowning of the old humanity came an epiphany. In its wake, "What the Thunder Said" inhabits a world that has been resurrected; it is a tale of remaking the world. It brings a new sense of justice, demanding that the human being must help each other. Violence must be ended and replaced by compassion and benevolence to bring back peace to the modern world, as it is seen in "Shantih, shantih, shantih" (Line, 433).

Eliot's poem can be seen not only over the span of five sections but also over the course of three days. Following Dante, the events of *The Waste Land* may be seen as having symbolically occurred between Good Friday and Easter Sunday. Thus, *The Waste Land* took place in the dark space between Christ's death and his resurrection three days later. The rain and the thunder serve as a prayer asking for God's help and protection to an arduous world-encompassing Mass (Hathaway, 53-4). The rain has fallen. It is refreshing and people are hopeful. Yet one should not forget the great sacrifices that come with this realization of God's help. In bringing in a new world order, Eliot is seemingly describing his contemporary world as utterly hopeless. As with Noah's flood renewal is seen in its wake, but only after complete destruction of the world by the flood. Phlebas' drowning ought to remind people of the cost of the quest, just as the tower of the "Hanged Man" in the last scene is a reminder of Christ's cross that was necessary for resurrection. However, in the aftermath there is much hope. The Fisher King spoke before in the past tense,

> "I sat upon the shore
> Fishing, with the arid plain behind me wondering
> Shall I at least set my lands in order?" (Lines, 423-5).

But he has left these dark thoughts of "dry brain in a dry season" behind, having been healed at last. By his help, the lands are also reclaimed. Perceval has found the Grail and survived the Chapel, and the king's mouth has been opened, before he could only silently fish and stew. He has been reborn, and the heroic cycle has been completed. Something new and positive has supplanted the old. The Fisher King, it would seem, is the central human character of the narrative, though he has little "screen time" in Eliot's poem. Yet, in the guise of the wounded king, Eliot has been working out his own salvation "with fear and trembling" (Philippians II.12). It seems only fitting that Christ shapes into his image of resurrection. Jesus himself, people recall, has some history with fish and fishing. At the beginning of Jesus' ministry he came upon two brothers, Andrew and Peter, fishing in a lake and called out to them, "'Come, follow me, and I will make you fishers of men'" (Matthew IV.19). Regardless of the theology involved, this image is directly translatable to the problem of the wasteland in modern society. Christ came to resurrect people's dead lives (metaphorically and otherwise) and the language of fishing makes Jesus' words applicable to modern Fisher King. Christ came to free people from dead-end lives, and to give them a new meaningful mission with meaning by showing them how to love others. Through his teaching, sacrifice, and rebirth, he has given his followers a new life, and Eliot uses the same picture to bring the Fisher King to life, along with all humanity. The Vedic Thunder and the resurrected Christ suggest the same message of rebirth. There is hope here for the emotionless men and women populating all wastelands in all times, whose spirits have dried up and deadened; "these fragments I have shored against my ruins" cries the Fisher King (Line, 430), and so should modern men. The memory of the quest for renewal becomes a shield against falling prey to such debilitating unfruitfulness again. Should anyone have to pass through the wasteland again, the memories here invoked prove that the quest can be completed again. Though perhaps not a cure, it is a preventative medicine to avoid the self-ruination of the human species. In *The Waste Land*, the stages of gloomy of human life have been experienced. Modern men have been through melancholy and despair, experienced the ineffectual rush of passion, giving way to misdirected desires, and fallen into resignation and despair. But Eliot refused to leave modern men in despair; he has shown them a new season, with which comes human recreation of, which denotes a rebirth into a new life. Like the Buddhist goal of escaping *samsara* or suffering, a new element is found to help modern man escape the everlasting cycle of sufferings. Modern man has ended in Purgatory, perhaps but Paradise is at least in sight and Hell is far behind, drowned in the sea. They are making their way up the mountain towards hope. That is what the "shantih, shantih, shantih" is there for, to overcome the fears and confusion with an everlasting peace. Here Eliot has found comfort and meaning for himself in the midst of a confused world. Perhaps modern man can manage the same thing.

If *The Waste Land* can be thought to have a "positive" message, it lies precisely in the strange negative strategy that aims to rescue modern man or perhaps only Eliot himself in that moment of desperation, from lack of moral, personal despair, and a new freedom in a modernity that increasingly seemed meaningless (Cooper, 2006: 68).

The Waste Land is a fragmented text. John Pawell Wards states,

> "There are different line-lengths; presence and absence of punctuation; clusters of capitals in italicized foreign tongues; short-word and long-word clusters; lexicons opulent and penurious; solid pentameter couplets and stabs of writing almost in collapse; and repetitions so frequent that we hardly reread them but more or less just see them again" (Ward, 2004: 336).

Eliot has deliberately chosen a complex technique to show that the problems are shared by all modern men wherever they are that is why he has written the poem in different languages, which can be considered as an indication of timelessness of the poem. It is an intuitive practice of the poet, who will not clumsily decide upon this or that letter's repetition or omission, even though that is occasionally possible. The repetition may imply that something occurs very often and omission may mean that a sort of problem is no longer there.

CHAPTER FOUR

The Image of The Modern Man in "The Hollow Men" and "Ash-Wednesday"

4.1. Modern Man as Hollow in "The Hollow Men" (1925)

It seems most logical to take up *The Hollow Men* (1925), after *The Waste Land* because it is closely related to *The Waste Land*. Grover Smith states that most of *The Hollow Men* is made up out of the lines Ezra Pound deleted from *The Waste Land*. No doubt, it has a strong thematic resemblance to *The Waste Land* like isolation, alienation and failure of communication, which one needs to first examine. The epigraph of *The Hollow Men* seems to be a reminder for even such monstrous men who at last believed in what they were doing, however horrific the results, setting up a natural contrast to the hollowness of modern man, who fundamentally believes in nothing and is, therefore, empty at the core of his being, like a Guy Fawkes dummy, if one bears in mind the well-known celebration in Valencia (Spain) (Kaplan, 1997: 51). So, two different types of "hollow/stuffed men" are presented: he who lacks a soul (Mister Kurtz) and he who lacks a real body (Guy Fawkes dummy), representing both physical and spiritual emptiness.

Sara Thorne states that *The Hollow Men* marks a spiritual low point in which the speaker represents a state of despair and emptiness (Thorne, 2006: 281); the poem mirrors the modern men, who lament their hollowness and their sense of life. They are not "lost violent souls," but only hollow men and stuffed with straw:

"We are the hollow men,
We are the stuffed men
Leaning together
Headpiece filled with straw. Alas!" (Lines, 1-4)

In death's "dream kingdom" the hollow men want to remain hollow and scarecrows-like; "Rat's coat, crowskin, crossed staves . . . ." They feared the reality of death, and the after-life as they had fear of the reality of this meaningless life in this world (Batra, 2001: 83-84).

George Williamson states that the title of the poem is derived from a combination of *The Hollow Land* by William Morris and *The Broken Men* by Kipling. Williamson also says that Geoffrey Tilloston, in his essays on Criticism and Research confirms that Eliot, himself has given the reader the expressions of his face. But it is easier to believe that it may have come from Shakespeare's Julius Caesar (IV. ii):

"When love begins to sicken and decay,
It useth an enforced ceremony.
There are no tricks in plain and simple faith;
But hollow men, like horses at hand,
Make gallant show and promise of their mettle;
But when they should endure the bloody spur,
They fall their crests, and, like deceitful jades,
Sink'in the trial."

If these are not the hollow men of Eliot's poem, they are very close to them that can raise questions in the mind of its readers (Williamson, 1953: 155).

B. C. Southam says that *The Hollow Men* is not an easy poem to annotate, though the language and imagery of the poem are simple. One does not face problems of historical reference or translation (Southam, 1968: 99). But the poem is highly allusive, which seems obscure and one cannot define Eliot's sources without some interpretation.

The world of the hollow men of this poem is the same as Prufrock's world (Eliot's Collected Poems, 1963: 89-92). Although it is a poem about the dilemmas of belief, *The Hollow Men* is explicitly about language. The modern men suffer from loss of faith, and loss of belief in themselves. Their suffering in the modern world makes their voices dried up and "quiet and meaningless" (Eliot's Collected Poems, 1963: 89). In the "broken jaw of our lost kingdom," they "avoid speech" (91). The journey, in *The Hollow Men*, towards the kingdom of life, through the three kingdoms of death, is an intensely personal and spiritual journey, but it has been made earlier by Dante; what Dante saw is, in fact, an interpretation of history (Jones, 1964: 152).

The language of the poem fails and mixes into the familiar sounds of childhood nursery rhymes as near the end of *The Waste Land* and yet they are strangely menacing. One is not surprised when it concludes in a defeated stammer:

> "voices are,
> In the wind's singing
> More distant and more solemn
> Than a fading star" (Lines, 25-28).

This distant lyricism cannot be heard in "the dead land", and neither can the "eyes" open wide on a visionary moment, "Sunlight on a broken column" (Line, 23). In anticipation of motions to come later in the 1920s, the speaker in the poem acknowledges hope as he trembles "with tenderness" and yearns for lips that would "kiss" and "Form prayers" (Line, 51). The modal here "would" defer faith, suspending belief, for the time being. In the moment of extreme doubt, the lines, that ask "Is it like this / In death's other kingdom", (Lines, 45-46) seem to render the visionary moment still more remote as the speaker considers the thoroughly distressing prospect that even no redemptive vision is possible "there." The depths of this despair cannot yet be plumbed. He goes away, and in section IV, he returns to the experiential realities of life in "this hollow valley" (Line, 55), classifying those things which are surely painful and unsatisfying. Subsequently, *Ash Wednesday, Journey of the Magi, Four Quartets*, and a series of Eliot's verse plays would return to the themes of faith and belief. But before the religious turn, Eliot would have to continue the journey through hell, which has begun with *The Love Song of J. Alfred Prufrock* (Cooper, 2006: 55-56).

Both, Kaplan and Williamson argue that the two epigraphs of *The Hollow Men* "Mistah Kurtz—he dead, and 'A penny for the Old Guy'", which are respectively taken from British tradition and Joseph

Conrad's novel, *Heart of Darkness*, point up the analogies at the centre of the poem. The two, Guy Fawkes and Kurtz are "lost violent souls" remembered now as "the hollow men . . . the stuffed men." In Conrad's *Heart of Darkness*, Marlow, the narrator, calls Kurtz "hollow at the core". Children carry about stuffed effigies of Guy Fawkes when they solicit (ask for money) "a penny for the Old Guy" (Kaplan, 1997: 51, and Williamson, 1953: 155). It is stated that the relation of this epigraph to the poem, however, suggests that as children make a game of make-believe out of Guy Fawkes, so one can make a similar game out of religion and the ritual game of the poem supports this implication (Williamson, 1953: 155).

Leonard Unger states that in *The Hollow Men* the themes of the fragmentation and the inarticulation are represented by both the form and the content of the statements. These themes are symbolized by a wealth of images, the most notable ones are "broken glass," "broken column," "broken stone," and "broken jaw." At the beginning of the poem, the voices of the hollow men "are quiet and meaningless," and towards the end their speech is broken into the Lord's Prayer;

> "For Thine is,
> Life is
> For Thine is the" (Lines, 90-92).

The Hollow Men is essentially Eliot's exploration of the state of his own soul as one of many modern souls suffering the same affliction of emptiness. It is an emptiness caused by the condition of the modern world, in which men live only for themselves, failing to choose between good and evil. The souls in the poem, whose condition, one is supposed to be horrified by, are not those who have sinned the most, but those who have not chosen whether or not to sin. They exist in a state in-between; a state in which their failure to make a decision causes an extreme lack of hope and joy or pain. The heroes of this poem are those who clearly see this state and recognize its true horror. Much of the horror of this state is constructed through the use of allusions that refer to past historical and fictitious characters who suffered similar fates, or who realized the horror of that fate in some decisive moments (Unger, 27: 1961). While Eliot's general intent may be clearly understood from the words of the poem, a much richer understanding can only be achieved by realizing the allusions he uses as literary tools to construct the work on a foundation laid by authors before him. The first and last passages of the final section are useless, immoral and evil parodies of children's game song.

Eliot concludes the poem by shortening and fracturing the final lines of the poem to emphasize the violent, meaningless struggle of modern men to transcend their mortal circumstances. So, *The hollow Men* is Eliot's vision of modern worshippers, filled with the "shadow" endemic to all men something between uninterested and a lack of conscience, and certainly the sense of prophesying of mortality. The poem also serves as the exact opposite for Eliot's "savior," the culture's representative killed ritually to secure the cultural and spiritual life of the tribe. After all, Guy Fawkes was put to death for his attempt to assassinate the Protestant king and Parliament; his execution and its reenactment each year provide a foundation for the Church of England's monopoly. Perhaps, Eliot also intends this apocalyptic and ironic poem to betray the unconsciously savage methods modern societies employ to fight or perpetuate the "shadow." Eliot's poem suggests, in fact, that the cure for cultural death and social alienation is worse than the disease. As Fawkes himself announces, "A desperate disease requires a dangerous remedy." In *The Hollow Men*, Eliot creates a multiple personality reminiscent of Gerontion: "stuffed men/ Leaning together/ Headpiece filled with straw," through which Eliot wants to highlight that the modern community is sterile, ineffectual, and incapable of meaning. As potential leaders of the modern culture, they represent the hollow men who have lived past their time; they are not good role models. Instead of giving voice to the decline of civilization and cultural soul, they have become the neurotic "victims" of a damaged and damaging nature. As they compare their utterances, for example, to "wind in dry grass" and "rats' feet over broken glass/In our dry cellar," they recall the opening of "A Game of Chess," as the husband silently derides, but his wife often complains to her husband's not answering her question. To her question, "What are you thinking of?" he answers, "I think we are in rats' alley/ Where the dead men lost their bones." The poet is no doubt referring to the emasculated condition of the "prophets" in his canon. Eliot suggests that they are unmanned, by the devouring public, represented by hungry, hysterical women: "Rachel née Rabinovitch," for instance, who "tears at the grapes with murderous paws" (Eliot's

Complete Poems and Plays, 1909-1950: 35), or the rank feline smell of "Grishkin in a drawing-room" (Eliot's Complete Poems and Plays:, 1909-1950: 33). Though there are no women characters in *The Hollow Men*, their enervating presence lurks in the hollow men's impotence, their failure to "mean" in this wrecked landscape. All humans, in fact, will return to nature's harsh womb, as in *Ash Wednesday,* as meaningless bones. *The Hollow Men* recalls the murderous sterility of scenes from Eliot's *The Waste Land,* where dogs dig up corpses from gardens, the cruel month of April breeds lilacs from the dead land, and the gurgle of the polluted river evokes worried visions of mortality in the Fisher King's abandoned son:

> "White bodies naked on the low damp ground
> And bones cast in a little low dry garret,
> Rattled by the rat's foot only, year to year"
> (Eliot's Complete Poems and Plays, 1909-1950: 43).

The horror that a frightened Eliot reports in *The Hollow Men* is indeed this noticeable lack of transcendence; an inability to "mean" anything. Like Dante's *Inferno,* Eliot's poetic vision records a surreal dream landscape hashed together from Biblical and medieval storehouses. The inhabitants of Eliot's hell on earth are sent to "Shape without form, shade without colour, / Paralyzed force gesture without motion" (Lines, 11-12). Eliot's poem describes it has turned into a kind of purgatory, where:

> "Those who have crossed
> With direct eyes, to death's other Kingdom
> Remember us—if at all—not as lost
> Violent souls, but only
> As the hollow men,
> The stuffed men" (Lines, 13-17).

To be remembered as violent, lost or even soulless as Kurtz would be better than to be forgotten. Memory is survival. Here Eliot suggests that the loss of voice and sight contribute to the disintegration of culture and perhaps leads to man's sense of alienation. People blinded themselves and neglected God. Vision, insight, and language are impaired. Those who cross over to "death's other Kingdom" pass with "direct eyes": they have seen what the hollow men refuse to, or dare not, see "Eyes I dare not meet in dreams" (Line, 19). Eliot makes a distinction in the poem between "death's other Kingdom," "the twilight kingdom," and "death's dream kingdom." This comparison implies that the hollow men are the living dead; they lack energy and seem to act without thinking as they are unaware of what is happening around them; and therefore, their only escape is into death's dreams, where the eyes they wish to avoid are transformed into images of classical decay, lost childhood and nature's triumph over civilization: "Sunlight on a broken column" or "a tree swinging." Perhaps Eliot critiques the impulse, born on the psychoanalyst's comfortable couch, to ascribe every neuroticism and unhappiness to an inner fault and to material in the unconscious death's dream kingdom, rather than to a fault in society, the ideology underlying that society, or the "god" that gives it shape. Eliot suggests that believing in the unconscious reliefs the modern citizen because it allows him to hide behind the "deliberate disguise" of the scavenger, death itself is: "Rat's coat, crowskin, crossed staves/ In a field/ Behaving as the wind behaves/ No nearer . . ." (Lines, 33-36). The unconscious is more comforting than God because it allows the hollow man to distance himself from that other kingdom: "And voices are/ In the wind's singing/ More distant and more solemn/Than a fading star" (Lines, 25-28). The hollow man wants to "be no nearer/ In death's dream kingdom" (Lines, 29-30), to "the eyes he dares not meet no nearer," that is to "that final meeting/ In the twilight kingdom." Eliot clearly identifies his poet with Guy Fawkes, who possessed the conviction of his beliefs for which he would kill and then was killed. After all, Mr. Fawkes rules over "the dead land" where "stone images are raised" to him and "receive/ The supplication of a dead man's hand" (Line, 43). Despite the bleak prospect, there is something uncannily, even surrealistically, sensual about this "supplication," the caress of this "dead man's hand" on the poet's supposedly dead libido. The poet wonders whether it will be the same in "earth's other kingdom," or whether he will again find himself "a king alone at the hour when we are / Trembling with tenderness," only to use "lips that would kiss" to "form prayers to broken stone" (57-58). This strange dream of failed transcendence, hard as it may try to condemn the empty motions that constitute it, eroticizes its failure. Impotence becomes coitus and interrupts, spiritual miscarriage

(MacDiarmid, 2003: 97). Eliot might here refer to his own inability to consummate or continue his marriage "saintliness" as he decided to live a celibate life. Therefore, he presents two failures at once, wallowing as any good moral masochist might in their ineffectual bids at spiritual supremacy.

Eliot's plans and arrangements for the poem are mysterious like his portrayal of the "perpetual star/ Multifoliate rose/ Of death's twilight kingdom" (Lines, 63-65). One may pose a question: does Eliot mean to suggest that incarnation and forgiveness in religion are impossible dreams? (Kaplan, 1997: 57), which Kaplan answered by examples from *Ash-Wednesday*, saying that "the aged eagle" is brought to the poem as a sort of indirect allusion to the Christians past life, and further explains that the eagle could suggest rebirth and renewal as an indication for baptism as a purification symbol.

His impressive lack serves as his power, and his sensual satisfaction. In fact,

> "In this last of meeting places
> We grope together
> And avoid speech
> Gathered on this beach of the tumid river
> Sightless, unless" (Lines, 57-61).

Eliot ends the poem with condemnation of all human intercourses, especially sexual, and again his repeated protestations and sermonizing reveal his interest in the subject:

> Between the idea
> And the reality
> Between the motion
> And the act
> Falls the Shadow
>   For Thine is the Kingdom
>   Between the conception
> And the creation
> Between the emotion
> And the response
> Falls the Shadow

Life is very long
Between the desire
And the spasm
Between the potency
And the existence
Between the essence
And the descent
Falls the Shadow
For Thine Is the Kingdom (Lines, 72-91)

Eliot eroticizes the sacrificial moment, as his "shadow" visits the sexual scene. Death is the third thing that penetrates every desiring moment; it is the regenerative spasm, the cruel orgasm, and God's unspeakable face. Thus pain and obliteration fuse with pleasure this awful moment of human intercourse, a vision of the Eternal Footman snickering at man's impotence. The Shadow decapitates the nursery rhyme and interrupts the Lord's Prayer, cutting off the big "bang" with a whimper, suffocating the hollow man's stuttering voice mid-prayer. In an uncanny fashion, Eliot implies that one can feel God's presence in his total absence, by the poet's inability and by the culture's lack of communication and moral:

"For Thine is
Life is
For Thine is the
This is the way the world ends
This is the way the world ends
This is the way the world ends
Not with a bang but a whimper" (Lines, 92-98).

The poet becomes silent by a whimper of masochistic cutting off and disconnecting. Russell Elliott Murphy comments that "Eliot's hollow men do not have the courage or the passion even to curse the darkness. Rather, they accept their self-willed fate, their pitiful tale ending, like the poem, "not with a bang but a whimper" (Murphy, 2007: 257). Eliot sums up the impression left by *The Hollow Men* best in his essay on Dante, as he describes the mental "state" that Dante creates in his Divine Comedy. Eliot says that Dante:

reminds us that Hell is not a place but a state, that man is damned or blessed in the creatures of his imagination as well as in men who have actually lived; and that Hell, though a state, is a state which can only be thought of, and perhaps only experienced, by the projection of sensory images; and that the resurrection of the body has perhaps a deeper meaning than we understand (Eliot's Selected Essays, 211-12).

Dante's is a visual imagination of a different sense from that of a modern painter of a still life: it is visual in the sense that he lived in an age in which men still believed in visions. It was a psychological habit, the trick which many people have forgotten. Modern men have nothing but dreams, and have forgotten that seeing visions and a practice now relegated to the aberrant and uneducated, was once a more significant, interesting, and disciplined kind of dreaming. (Eliot's Selected Essays, 204).

Eliot's allusive sources are well chosen, for they bring to mind examples of souls which suffer from the same moral condition as those in the poem. All of those souls that are referenced are taken from works or events that are extremely powerful. Eliot's use of them adds considerably to the power that his poem can convey. From *The Devine Comedy*, he takes images of souls at every level of the afterlife: hell, purgatory, and heaven. Dante's lost souls, which never made up their minds to live their lives for good or evil, are denied entrance; therefore, all the three places: hell, purgatory and heaven have the same condition as the modern life. Dante the pilgrim becomes heroic in that he dares to look at his guilt, shame, and sin and then makes the conscious decision repent. Joseph Conrad's Kurtz is also able to recognize this danger, because in his death he realizes the horror of the modern life, while Marlow, who also realizes a bit of the danger, cannot bring himself to face the truth of it. Guy Fawkes's whimper spells the end of the failed conspiracy with which he was involved. By doing so, he gives up the choice he made for rebellion. The tragedy of the modern man in *The Hollow Men* is intensified because it is presented within the context of possible ultimate meaning: "it gives the complete impression, not that life as a whole is meaningless, but it has a purpose which the hollow men refuse to acknowledge, and it is, therefore, meaningless for them" (Sullivan, 1973: 49).

Without these specific examples, Eliot could not convey the same meanings that he wanted to express. In this poem, the allusions do not present particularly strong examples of the condition Eliot is conveying, but they add to the power of the poem considerably by evoking a sense of history, of being part of something larger, of a continual decline, or of a constant danger of the human condition. The whimper with which the world ends is the whimper of modern man, the whimper of Guy Fawkes giving away other members of his plot; Brutus betraying Caesar, Kurtz finally seeing all that he has created and been a part of for what it is, and the murmur of the shades which can never enter heaven or hell. Seen in this context, the last words of the poem gain a sort of power they do not have on their own, as they echo the spirits of other historical and fictitious characters. Only by discovering the sources of Eliot's allusions, one can come to a complete understanding of the poem, regardless of how well it may appear to stand on its own.

Eliot himself gives very clear clues to at least two of his allusive sources by direct quotations before the poem begins: first in the epigraph to the section, taken directly from *Heart of Darkness*, and then in the epigraph to the poem, taken from the children's cry on Guy Fawkes Day. These are not clearly meant to be hidden references and once they are discovered, other uses of those sources and other sources that touch upon the same themes can be quickly discovered and interpreted. Perhaps, *The Hollow Men* communicates more immediately than *The Waste Land* because it is less ambitious in form and as a result more easily grasped as a whole and it also has a greater unity and organization, which reflect Eliot's firmer conviction of the importance of that spiritual attitude (Sullivan, 1973: 49).

4.2. The Image of Modern Man in "Ash-Wednesday" (1930)

The title of the poem implies that Eliot has moved towards Christianity. In fact, *Ash-Wednesday* is a name given to the Christian's forty days of fasting, which is an indication of turning from sin moving towards faith that precedes the Easter celebration of Christ's resurrection (Herbert, 1982: 41). It is said that as a Christian ritual, the priest dips his thumb in ashes and marks the sign of the cross on his forehead while he "intones": "Remember, man that thou art dust, and unto dust thou shalt return." The speech of the priest is to warn the modern man of the uselessness of their being too busy with this materialistic life and ignore their faith, man forget about their God; thus, it urges man to return to God (Williamson, 1957: 168). Kaplan also states that the poem, *Ash-Wednesday* is about the day in which "Christians ask God's help to turn back from the temptations and evils of the world and the flesh" (Kaplan, 1997: 56). Sencourt suggests that "it is only the total effect of *Ash-Wednesday*, which is capable of systematic exposition." (Sencourt, 2005: 144) If this is indeed the case, then what Kirk believes to be the essential thrust of the poem proves helpful:

> Only by experiencing afresh the reality that once brought forth the old symbols can modern man regain faith, the substance of things hoped for, and the evidence of things unseen. Just that expression anew of transcendent experience was Eliot's achievement in Ash-Wednesday (Kirk, 1971: 178)

Indeed *Ash-Wednesday* had a considerable positive religious impact on the way people were perceiving Christianity and communism since the poem "made it possible to believe in Christian insights and yet to remain within the pale of modern intellectuality." (Samuel Hynes, 2006: 64) Eliot himself was the paragon of such a posture. A man of genuine intellectual power and broad learning might experience something of the transcendent, and might express that experience in a mingling of old and new symbols (Kirk, 1971: 179).

Sullivan states that Jones. E. E. has said that the themes of introspection, solitariness and despair are of the most important themes of *Ash-Wednesday*, which are the main features of the modern man in the poem. When man realizes his sins and thought that he was in a wrong path in the world then he feels sad and unhappy for he was neglecting God and turned to the world. Eliot in the first three lines of the poem suggests a kind of repentance for the previous sins:

> "Because I do not hope to turn again
> Because I do not hope
> Because I do not hope to turn" (Lines, 1-3)

The above lines denote that the speaker in the poem has decided to give up the world and turn to God. The poet says: "Desiring this man's gift and that man's scope/ I no longer strive to strive towards such things" (Lines, 4-5), Eliot no longer likes the trivial wishes and hopes that is why he has converted to Christian religion and his hope to take the other world as more important (Sullivan, 1973: 50)

Ash-Wednesday causes problem for Eliot's critics. While they agree that the mythical or occult method, borrowed from Joyce and enhanced with Frazer's myths, characterizes much of Eliot's work including *Ash-Wednesday;* they claim, as does Linda Leavell, that this poem "seems to elude explication, especially an explication based on allusions" (MacDiarmid, 2003: 98). Drawing on his impressions of Dante's accessible universality, Eliot claims that an allegorical, or visual method, which is detached from immediate meaning is the most vivid and disciplined kind of dreaming, available to poets and readers. In short, Eliot's mysterious poem describes a mystic set of visions that he claims come from above rather than below, whereas Leavell describes the method she finds in *Ash-Wednesday* as the "ritual method", "a projection from immediate meaninglessness towards the infinite unknowable, the ineffable name," or the future, which she claims is an amalgamation of mythic and nonsense methods (MacDiarmid, 2003: 99).

Linda Leavell asserts that *Ash-Wednesday* celebrates the impending horror and modern man's inability to understand or fill that sort of horror, and argues that "The poem requires explication no more than the finest nonsense verse," and "yet it holds just beyond our grasp, a meaning more profound than perhaps any in modern poetry." Eliot's instrument of self-torture is just not finely calibrated in his earlier poems. That is, he has not yet created his most sensual hell. His work on that score is more obvious in *Ash-Wednesday,* as Leavell points out in her essay, who emphasizes her claim a step further concluding "While the rhythm of *Ash-Wednesday* suggests a liturgy", it is "truly a common prayer, its ritual runs deeper than Anglicanism, deeper even than Christianity, as deep as man's primal cry to his Maker" (Leavell, 1988: 152).

Like *The Love Song, Ash-Wednesday* is also a dramatic monologue. The protagonist in the poem plunged into hopelessness. Like the earlier poems, *Ash-Wednesday* focuses on the conflict between the values of the flesh and those of the spirit, where the latter is shown in terms of a quest for union with the word. The dream women in part IV, is the symbol of salvation, while she is never identified. It may be possible that on the one hand she is identified with the Virgin and on the other hand with Beatrice of Dante's *Purgatorio*. She serves, through her double role, to unite the divine and the human. In part I, when the protagonist who is deprived of her presence is unable to turn towards her, while she may be an object of desire. This means, symbolically he is cut off from love of both human and divine (Kaplan, 1997: 57)

Leavell's reading contradicts the critical difficulties occasioned by Eliot's complete change from a witty and ironic allusiveness to a deadly investigation of the "mysteries." Leavell shows that Hugh Kenner, in his *Invisible Poet,* marks *Ash-Wednesday* as a dividing line for Eliot. While his language in his earlier poems tended towards a certain kind of difficulty and complexity (Leavell, 1988: 152).

Ash-Wednesday is Eliot's analytical and personal poem, which is concerned with his own religious conversion. This is partly considered as a study of the way a highly poetic and intellectual mind attempts to focus on an uninteresting and ordinary considerations and earthly doubts in order that the spirit may obtain salvation. "But his honesty is so great that poem is more a cry imploring grace, a plea for pardon and redemption through the church". The poem starts with a statement of the change in his previous attitudes of his decision not to return to the glory of life, and at the end of the first section he ends his prayer by asking for God's mercy. Eliot as a modern man is "convinced of his unworthiness and his need for repentance" (Anderson and Walton, 1949: 1240). It is the continuation of the self-flagellating stutters that terminate *The Hollow Men:*

> "Because I do not hope to turn again . . . /
> Desiring this man's gift and that man's scope
> I no longer strive to strive towards such things
> (Why should the aged eagle stretch its wings?)
> Why should I mourn
> The vanished power of the usual reign?" (Lines, 1-8)

There is certainly something disturbing and embarrassing to Eliot's change in pace, poetic material and tone. His humble protestations seem like the hand-wringing self promotions of a latter-day. The impulse to dismiss such sermonizing as the usual aged nonsense, a 51-year-old man passing himself off as a dying sage is overpowering. Richard Aldington only did this in his 1931 comic novel, *Stepping Heavenward,* where he describes a mid-western saint's purgatorial journey through England with his neurotic wife. The novel is a barely veiled attack on Eliot for his conversion, his holier-than-thou attitude, and his fascination with the moral and physical masochism of the saints. *Ash-Wednesday* is perhaps Eliot's first overtly and, for some, regrettably confessional poem. Its obvious Catholic material suggests, to a traitorous alliance. The converted Eliot becomes the Guy Fawkes of modern literature, described as the pathetic neurotic rather than the sacrificial lamb which he wanted to be. *Ash-Wednesday* explodes, in a sense, the established themes and sentiments of the mythic method that Eliot claims to admire in Joyce. In 1902, Joyce wrote to Lady Gregory to complain that "there is no heresy or no philosophy which is very abhorrent to my church as a human being," and to share with her his resultant manifesto:

> I shall try myself against the powers of the world. All things are inconstant except the faith of the soul, which changes all things and fills their inconstancy with light. And though I seem to have been driven out of my country here as a misbeliever I have found no man yet with a faith like mine (Joyce, 1957: 53).

In *Ash-Wednesday,* it is evident that the modern man is spiritually barren and in quest for moral purification. Religion is the best possible solution for him. It represents the struggle of any devotee in the modern time. Here a devotee struggles to go through self-examination, self-exploration, penitence and move towards the path of spirituality. Eliot appears to embrace the church and its police, tax men, and jailers as he turns his back, once and for all, on any alliance with his home country. He pledges his allegiance to anti-humanistic tyranny at the expense of his, and by implication our, very "being." Joyce's reliance upon Dionysian structures of myth and meaning serves as a deliberate rejection of the orthodox structure in Ireland, a country which he abandons in part because of its complicity in its own political and religious subjection: "I will tell you what I will do and what I will not do," says Stephen Dedalus:

> I will not serve that in which I no longer believe, whether it call itself my home, my fatherland, or my church; and I will try to express myself in some mode of life or art as freely as I can and as wholly as I can, using for my defence the only arms I allow myself to use, silence, exile and cunning (A Portrait of The Artist As A Young Man, 1914: 241).

Eliot turns his back on the freedom of Joyce's private, polytheistic mythology in order to pay obedience to his fatherland and most importantly, in Eliot's estimation to a national Church. Perhaps *Ash-Wednesday* is unsettling because it renounces the artistic goals that the younger Eliot following Joyce so fervently espouses. Old Eliot is no longer the rebel, lighting out for the territories of surrealism, free verse and the red-light district of Paris. Instead, he "sells out" to the establishment what seems like a mouthful of mud (MacDiarmid, 2003: 105).\

Dennis Brown states that *Ash-Wednesday* constitutes an appealingly desperate confession. It has a continuous mourning for "the lost heart", which also seeks ". It seems to be a deliberate willed project to give up will to power:

> Because these wings are no longer wings to fly
> But merely vans to beat the air . . . /
> Teach us to care and not to care
> To us to sit still. (Lines, 35-36 and 39-40).

According to Brown this is a sort of renunciation of selfhood in relation with others like the reader as well as God and invoked spiritual helpers (Brown, 2003: 4).

There is a similarity between modern man and *Ash*-Wednesday, because it is hard to find sense in both of them. That is why Eliot wrote the poem to depict the image of modern man. There is no sense in *Ash-Wednesday*, for instance, Eliot plans to continue the struggle to create the uncreated conscience of his race in his own soul, or even to move towards the establishment of a body of occult knowledge privy to the chosen few. Rather, Eliot drops one of his characteristic poetic masks; he no longer poses as the anti-Romantic, the exiled cultural arbiter. In contrast to his early works, *Ash-Wednesday* is embarrassingly free of dishonest behaviour, of a trick to achieve its goal of succinct impenetrability. Eliot is no longer playing his contemporaries' game. Or if he is, he's doing it at a deeper, more cunning level. His confession is a personal affront to the modern readership because it indicts not only his own artistic sins but those of his intellectual generation. Eliot proudly proclaims his impotence as a triumphant over the vain "glory" of his peers. The meek shall inherit the afterlife:

> "Because I do not hope to know again
> The infirm glory of the positive hour
> Because I do not think
> Because I know I shall not know
> The one veritable transitory power
> Because I cannot drink . . .
> I renounce the blessed face
> And renounce the voice . . .
> And pray to God to have mercy upon us
> May the judgment not be too heavy upon us
> Because these wings are no longer wings to fly
> But merely vans to beat the air . . .
> Pray for us sinners now and at the hour of our death
> Pray for us now and at the hour of our death."
> (Eliot's Complete Poems and Plays: 1909-1950: 60-61)

Eliot's literality prevents the reader the joy, or expectation, of his personal discovery. Eliot's *Ash-Wednesday* is written in something like bad faith, since "we don't have the words for this concept of communion now . . . That is why Pound has to be so indirect, why he can't simply tell us" (Crane-Ross, 1979: 201), what he means. In other words, Eliot's method short-circuits the individual impression of the sacred marriage that Pound tackles so obliquely in Canto 81 in favour of the cliché. Eliot's *Ash-Wednesday* is uneasy after the fashion because it's the kind of difficulty we enjoy. It flatters our self-esteem (Carne-Ross, 1979: 216). The poet thinks that he is old now and spent his life in a secular world, which never wishes to return to it again, moreover, he repeats the phrase "pray for us" since he realizes that he is sinful and as a kind of purgatory from the sins.

In Eliot's work, Frye claims, "religion forms a third level above human society" (Frye, 1963: 22). Eliot can only second such motions when he reminds readers that in Dante's time Europe, with all its dirtiness was mentally more united than the modern man can now conceive (Eliot's Selected Essays, 1950: 202). Lyndall Gordon describes Eliot's treasonous move as a return to a Victorian sensibility: "While most of the postwar generation liberated itself from faith," she writes, "Eliot moved in the opposite direction. The moderns rebelled against a Victorian version of faith, full of cant and hypocrisy. Eliot held on to an older faith, which was passionate and mystical" (Eliot's Early Years, 1973: 103). Many people in the twentieth century became irreligious because they thought that Churches no longer have power to bring peace back to the modern world but Eliot was different and turned to Christian religion and considers it as a sort of solution for all the problems of the modern man.

Eliot's turn to religious sensibility is a turn away from the modernist ethic which is described and spread by such energetic New World salesmen. In every case, an oppressive narrative voice breaks in taking the name of God and speaking in Biblical tones, in order to dictate the terms of the relationship between the speaker and the spoken. Eliot's artistic communion, is then, not constructive or empowering. Though Eliot frequently alludes to Christ's passion, crucifixion and resurrection, it would be very great pride and belief in his own importance to suggest that he identifies himself with Christ. Rather, Eliot stresses the poet's unimportance as compared to himself when he was baptized. (MacDiarmid, 2003: 104). Eliot believed that his poetry became more powerful after his conversion to Christianity, as if, that change in his life brought him a spiritual relief and power to enable him write poem better like *The Four Quartets*.

Though Eliot may not have read any particular passage of Frazer's *Golden Bough* when he writes *Ash-Wednesday,* his imagery of the "the mute Lady of the garden who sits "between the slender/Yew trees" recalls Frazer's account. In particular, the initiate of liveliness in sexual strength seems demanded by the Lady god who has been "offended" by "these bones":

> "Lady, three white leopards sat under a juniper-tree
> In the cool of the day, having fed to satiety
> On my legs my heart my liver and that which had been
>   contained
> In the hollow round of my skull. And God said
> Shall these bones live? Shall these
> Bones live? And that which had been contained
> In the bones (which were already dry) said chirping:
> "Because of the goodness of this Lady
> And because of her loveliness, and because
> She honors the Virgin in meditation,
> We shine with brightness. And I who am here dissembled
> Proffer my deeds to oblivion, and my love
> To the posterity of the desert and the fruit of the gourd"
> (Eliot's Complete Poems and Plays: 1909-1950: 61)

This is a bloodless "Day of Blood", a destruction of personality and memory rather than body, a mutilation of mind. In *Ash-Wednesday,* Eliot reestablishes the gulf between subject and God, by glorifying in God's ability to destroy him completely. Masculinity, intention, and virility are definitely on the chopping block, as the narrative voice, a "withered apple seed," surrenders to the Lady and becomes one with the garden. The poem takes on a series of complete opposite ideas in addition to the division between self and other, or poet/creator and God; the poem tackles the gap between male and female, mind and body, divine and human, saved and damned. Eliot's simultaneous opposing feeling about his "fortunate fall", the idea that in order to become moral, the weak subject must first discover himself to be damned, appears in his portrayal of the silent Lady is like the shadow of *The Hollow Men*, which is represented as a silent body, she is no longer Eliot's material Lamia, as in *Portrait of a Lady*. Instead, she is a saint whose presence speaks of a divine yet absent father. Her abstract sensuality is connected to the vision and clarity in "the dream crossed twilight between birth and dying" (Eliot's Complete Poems and Plays,

1909-1950: 66). Her body is a mystical space, as it transforms sexual longing into eroticized intuition of God:

> "And the lost heart stiffens and rejoices
> In the lost lilac and the lost sea voices
> And the weak spirit quickens to rebel
> For the bent golden-rod and the lost sea smell
> Quickens to recover
> The cry of quail and the whirling plover
> And the blind eye creates
> The empty forms between the ivory gates
> And smell renews the salt savour of the sandy earth."
> (Eliot's Complete Poems and Plays, 1909-1962: 66)

This Lady in the poem "who honuors the Virgin in mediation, the spirit of the river, spirit of the sea," becomes "all women" in this poem. As the poet's object of meditation, this "enlightened" virgin transforms his earthly longings into proper sensations, bringing him to the "place of solitude where three dreams cross." Eliot's poem describes a cosmic orgasm and ends in the promise of the crashing (MacDiarmid, 2003: 98-105). Kaplan comments on the way the image of woman is delineated, he says that a woman in *Ash-Wednesday* is no longer only a fertility symbol but she is raised to a spiritual level on which her sexuality has become blended with her spirituality. Thus, the poem can be regarded as an allegory of the relation of modern man to the church because woman becomes a symbol of more than mere sexuality and reunion with her is actually a step forward in the process of achieving union with "The Word" (Kaplan, 1997: 57). In this poem women's role is enhanced which indicates that they are developed in the society. They are no longer function as a mere machine as they were in The Waste Land or useless characters in The Love Song who only wasted their time by talking about trivial matters, such as their talking about Michaelangelo.

In fact, in *Ash Wednesday* Eliot partially rescinds his interests in the "Dionysian", replacing untamed celebration with "worried repose." The poem asks about the value that it teaches people to sit still rather than to dance in celebration of the mystical meeting. The poet's purpose is simply to witness a series of merged opposites that gesture at the impossible presence between them. They all describe the sinful modern man whose speech must only be repentance because death is the end of all people, and death is life since it ends with an eternal life as seen in:

> "end of the endless
> Journey to no end
> Conclusion of all that
> Is inconclusible
> Speech without word and
> Word of no speech"
> (Eliot's Complete Poems and Plays, 1909-1950: 62).

Eliot's divine unity is not Dionysus' extreme sensuality but an emotional desert:

> "Under a juniper-tree the bones sang, scattered and
>   shining
> We are glad to be scattered, we did little good to each
>   other,
> Under a tree in the cool of the day, with the blessing
>   of sand,
> Forgetting themselves and each other, united
> In the quiet of the desert. This is the land which ye
> Shall divide by lot. And neither division nor unity
> Matters. This is the land. We have our inheritance."
> (Eliot's Complete Poems and Plays, 1909-1950: 62-63)

Eliot connects all kinds of human intercourses, sexual, conversational, and intellectual with false turns on the path to the divine dream. In Part III, he compares his last-long conversion process to a staircase; at each turn he blinds himself to the distractions set in his way. For instance, he climbs past the "devil of the stairs who wears/ The deceitful face of hope and of despair" (Line, 63-64), eschewing human emotions. Then, at the "second stair," he rejects sexual congress as he turns his back on a horrific gynecological image: "Damp, jagged, like an old man's mouth drivelling, beyond repair, / Or the toothed gullet of an aged shark" (Eliot's Complete Poems and Plays, 63).

These images contain Eliot's fears of a devouring female sexuality; his deliberate blindness to them is a celebration of male impotence and, in a perverse way. Finally, Eliot turns his back at the Dionysian dance as an even more a very harmful danger than the desiring woman. The dance promises the pregnant erotic, that is:

> "At the first turning of the third stair
> Was a slotted window bellied like the fig's fruit
> And beyond the hawthorn blossom and a pasture scene
> The broad backed figure drest in blue and green
> Enchanted the may time with an antique flute.
> Brown hair is sweet, brown hair over the mouth blown,
> Lilac and brown hair;
> Distraction, music of the flute, stops and steps of the
>   mind over the third stair,
> Fading, fading, strength beyond hope and despair
> Climbing the third stair."
> (Eliot's Complete Poems and Plays, 1909-1950: 63)

Pastoral images are further deceits, disguises for a fertility that will detain the poet from his quest. Eliot blocks them all out with having a tendency to belittle himself to Lord's Prayer: "Lord, I am not worthy// but speak the word only".

Eliot unites his unspoiled hyacinth girl with the sun god, transforming her into pure fetish. Eliot's choice of the "silent sister veiled in white and blue" over the music of the flute not only redeems the time but the woman as well. By installing her in his poetry as the symbol of the word unheard, unspoken, who "signs but speaks no word," Eliot masks her pathological potential, erases the damaging reputation of original sin from her. A sketch rather than a human being, she can no longer dictate the terms of the conversation, or insert herself in the poet's dream as the portrait of a laughing Medusa, a toothed gullet. As the anti-Vivien, the lady in *Ash-Wednesday* forgives the "love unsatisfied" made worse by Eliot's marriage and allows him to escape from his sick wife. Eliot's marital and religious crises were inseparably mixed. Gordon says; "through his impulsive love of Vivien, Eliot made that frightful discovery of morality" when "the not naturally bad but irresponsible and undeveloped nature is caught in the consequences of its own action and becomes moral only by becoming damned." Thus Eliot celebrates his failure as the beginning of grace. Gordon continues and says,

> The sense of damnation, the remorse and guilt that Vivien evoked were essential to Eliot's long purgatorial journey. He could escape from her morally only by avoiding physical pleasure and living a simple life for religious reasons (Eliot's Early Years, 1973: 123).

One may say that the reasons behind Eliot's conversion to Christian religion are his wife's sickness and the results of the destructive World Wars. Eliot may represent that type of modern man who ascribed the entire problems of the modern society to their ignoring of God but instead of that they consider the secular world more important. Eliot believed that the physical pleasure is a hindrance in front of the modern man to turn to God that is why he has decided to live a simple life and devote himself for religion and to be far from his wife.

As a would-be saint, Eliot worships the woman but cannot touch her. Frye's estimation of Eliot's longing for the medieval mindset is perhaps dead on the mark; such unfairness and injustice, Lacan reminds people, joins the wound over the lack of the sexual union by pretending that it is people who have put it there. The offended woman is converted, in the chivalric fantasy and in Eliot's confessional poem, from laughing Medusa's head to the Father's intercessor:

> "Will the veiled sister between the slender
> Yew trees pay for those who offend her
> And are terrified and cannot surrender
> And affirm before the world and deny between the rocks
> In the last desert between the last blue rocks
> The desert in the garden the garden in the desert
> Of drouth, spitting from the mouth the withered
>   apple-seed"
> (Eliot's Complete Poems and Plays, 1909-1962: 65-66).

The Lady's job is to affirm "the desert in the garden and the garden in the desert." She does this by "spitting from the mouth the withered apple-seed" that is not only the sign of original sin but of the withered man and his impotent seed. She "forgives" all Eliot's offenses, then. The woman in Eliot's poem turns from self-interest and sexuality to self-sacrifice and sublimation, a move that creates the cult of true womanhood is first completed, as Christianity reconstructs the Great Mother as the Virgin Mary and thus idealizes maternity. Eliot repeats this conversion in *Ash-Wednesday*. Eliot writes, "I rejoice", then, "having to construct something/ Upon which to rejoice" (Eliot's Complete Poems and Plays, 1909-1950: 61). Eliot feels happy by his conversion because he repeats it more than twice, as if, he is completely removed from his earlier sins, and his repetition of his conversion is a kind attracting the attention of the those who read his poems generally and *Ash-Wednesday* in particular.

Eliot's religious poetry works very powerfully, as Eliot uses his new and improved Lady to represent the silent garden where the poet's word is born. Thus Eliot recasts her as a portal to what one might call the before-and-after-life: she offers, through the simple contemplation of her bright, voiceless body, the poet's means of escape or return to a lost unity. Some might interpret this as Eliot's longing after an unmediated relationship to the mother what is called the abject. Eliot portrays this state, however, as a merging with pre-history or even pre-time, an infinite return to a previous worse state to a wordless logo. If one can call it Eliot's dream of pure or perfect kind treatment, it must be a bodiless mothering, since one must admit that Eliot wants to go after an unmediated relationship with God (MacDiarmid, 2003: 108-112). The Lady who is mentioned in the poem is considered as the Christian Great Mother, she is least or most alienated from the reins of phallic power and so is unlikely to take revenge on the poet for what she sees as his original crime: his birth, for her a paradoxical love satisfied and unsatisfied.

Finally, it is clear that *Ash-Wednesday* is more than an exercise of a modern man in piety or in psychological narrative of the progress of the soul concerning the previous sins that he has committed in his life. As Rajan argues that this poem is an exploration of how paradise is lost, it obtains much of its power and some of its weight of unhappiness of a previous continuing effort to rediscover paradise, which one can say that in *Ash-Wednesday* it reaches its climax and its betrayal (Rajan, 1976: 70).

CONCLUSION

Eliot has depicted the image of modern man throughout his poetry as a changeable image. In the beginning of his career as a poet, Eliot tried hard to understand the entire problems of modern man. He believed that the unsolved problems of the modern society are many, for instance Prufrock who is the representative of modern man, is a character, which lacks the courage to speak. He is afraid to talk with the ladies who were busy with trivial things like talking about Michaelangelo that also indicates that modern man is wasting his time. He is aimless and has a sense of being lost, as Prufrock says they "talked for an hour" (Line. 11), purposelessly.

The way Eliot portrayed the modern man indicates that modern man can be divided into two different groups; one is conscious of his own problems and others problems like Prufrock, but can not solve them. The second group is unaware of such problems. An example for this group of modern people is the women who are very careless and unaware of their own problems. Prufrock is the example of those who are aware of their problems but is unable to express them that is why he remains sad and pessimist throughout *The Love Song*.

Eliot's poems mirror the different stages of Eliot's life. For instance, Prufrock reflects the earlier period of Eliot's life because there are some indications in the poem, which show that, when Eliot was in Paris, he was very fond of the ladies i.e., the ladies who were living in cheap hotels. He wanted to have a close relationship with them but his physical appearance does not allow him to have a close relationship with them. Perhaps, even the "sea-girls" in the line before the last line of *The Love Song* are the same ladies that he has seen in Paris. Modern man is shown as a hesitant character that could be compared to Hamlet or John the Baptist. Both Hamlet and John the Baptist were successful, but on the contrary modern man failed since he did not dare to sing his love song. In *The Waste Land*, the problems of modern man have become worse because of the negative and harsh effects of the First World War on the life of people but the poet is striving to find the causes of his spiritual dilemma. Eliot believes that all the problems of modern man are because of their neglecting God, like when he says: "come in under the shadow of this red rock," which indicates that if the modern man turns to God and neglects the materialistic world, his problems would be solved.

The Waste Land shows another stage of Eliot's life. He had many problems during the time of composing the poem. The poem indicates that life has lost its true value; the peace of mind is lost, people became selfish, love did not have its meaning, marriage, which is only a bond between the wife and the husband, has lost its real meaning, human being was considered as machines, modern man became Godless, the relationship between the members of the family became very weak, the modern city resembled a desert where life was quite gloomy. Modern man lost has lost his values especially women by only looking after children, many of them turned to prostitution because they did not have any source of income; therefore, they used that as a way to earn money to maintain life. These are the characteristics of the modern city, which are shared by all the countries, especially Europe. Eliot insists on the necessity of turning from world to God. He believed that God can solve their problems, because man or any other earthly power could not change that gloomy and aimless life, which modern man complained against.

In *The Hollow Men*, the modern man realised that he is spiritually hollow. The modern man is like Kurtz, who did not realise what he did. He deified himself, tortured people and created them as slaves but on his death he attained self-realisation of the horror he had created when he says, "the horror, the horror the horror!", which denotes the moment of his late self-discovery. If Conrad's story ends with Kurtz's self-realisation, Eliot's The Hollow Men starts with modern man's self-discovery and then the modern man repents and asks for God's help and surrenders to God, he does not intend to do the same thing he used to do in the past.

Ash-Wednesday presents the confirmation of Eliot's repentance from his earlier sins. Modern man in this stage wants to be very religious and repent for his sins, which is a condition for his repentance to be accepted. Modern man is very hopeful like "the aged eagle" which can renew itself in water and sun. Finally Ash-Wednesday indicates that there is hope for those people who were involved with deadly sins in their life. They can be baptised which indicates spiritual purgation.

Throughout Eliot's poems it is clear that Eliot has realised all the modern problems of life as a very conscious poet and even suggests solutions for them. The only solution for the entire problems of modern man is to turn to God and neglect the world that completely occupied them spiritually.

Eliot has succeeded to depict the exact image of modern man. He has tried hard to transfer to the new generation what has happened in the twentieth century. All of his poems especially *The Waste Land* have shown readers all the aspects of the modern life. Life is depicted as a mirror, broken and shattered into pieces as it is clear in the different parts of the poem. Eliot unlike many poets did not leave the modern man lost in despair but he finds that the modern man could find his psychic peace and stability faith and a true turning to God.

BIBLIOGRAPHY

Abrams M. H., Donalson E, Talbot Adams, Robert. M. Monk, Samuel Holt Lipking, Lawrence Ford, George. H. Daiches David and Smith Hallet.

The Norton Anthology of English Literature, 4th.ed, New York, London: George J. McLeod Limited, W. W. Norton and Company, Inc. 2000.

Anderson George Kumler and Walton Eda Lou. *This generation: a selection of British and American literature from 1914 to the Present*, Princeton: Princeton University, 1949.

Asher Kenneth. *T.S. Eliot and Ideology*, Cambridge: Cambridge University Press, 1998.

Ayers David. *Modernism: A Short Introduction*, Oxford: Blackwell Publishing, 2004.

Balmar *Randall. Religion in Twentieth Century America*, Oxford, New York: Oxford University Press, 2001.

Batra Shakti. *T.S. Eliot: A Critical Study of his Poetry*, New Delhi: Ivy, 2001.

Beach Christopher. *The Cambridge Introduction to Twentieth-Century American Poetry*, Cambridge: Cambridge University Press, 2003.

Beasley Rebecca. *Theorists of Modernist Poetry: T.S. Eliot, T.E. Hulme and Ezra Pound*, New York: Routledge, 2007.

Bedenhausen Richard. *T.S. Eliot and the Art of Collaboration*, Cambridge: Cambridge University Press, 2004.

Bell, Michael. *Literature, Modernism and Myth, Belief and Responsibility in the Twentieth Century*, Cambridge: Cambridge University Press, (N.D)

Berghaus Günter. *International futurism in arts and literature*, Berlin: de Gruyter 2000.

Blistein Burton. *The design of The Waste Land*, Chicago: Loyola University Press, 2008.

Brown Richard Danson & Gupta Suman. *20ʰ Century Aestheticism & Modernism*, London: Routledge University Press, 2005.

Burns Allan. *Thematic Guide to American Poetry*, London: Greenwood Press, 2002.

Carl Woodring & Shapiro James. *The Columbia History of British Poetry*, New York: Columbia University Press, 1994.

Cervo Nathan. A. *Eliot's The Love Song of J. Alfred Prufrock*, ProQuest Direct Complete. Molly Hoff, San Antonio, Texas 60.4. (Summer, 2002): p.207.

Childs Donald. J. *Modernism and eugenics, Woolf, Eliot, Yeats and the culture of Degeneration*, Cambridge: Cambridge university Press, 2004.

Childs Peter. *Modernism*, London and New York: Routledge, 2000.

Cooper John Xiros. *The Cambridge Introduction to T.S. Eliot*, Cambridge: Cambridge University Press, 2006.

Cox C. B. and A. E. Dyson. *Modern Poetry, Studies in Practical Criticism: Yeats to Eliot*, London: Edward Arnold, 1978.

—and Hinchliffe Arnold. P. *T.S. Eliot: The waste Land*, London: Macmillan, 1968.

Cronin Richard, Chapman Alison and Harrison Antony. H. *A Companion to Victorian poetry*, Oxford: Blackwell, 2002.

Cuddy Lois A. *T.S. Eliot and the poetics of evolution: sub/versions of classicism, Culture and Progress*, London: Associated University Press, 2000.

Dame Helen Louise Gardner, *The Waste Land 1972: the Adamson Lecture, 3ʳᵈ, May, 1972*. Manchester: University of Manchester Press, 1972.

Damrosch David, and Dettmar Kevin J. H. *Longman Anthology of British Literature*, vol.2. London: Pearson Longman, 2006.

Dutton Richard. *An Introduction to Literary Criticism*, Longman: York Press, 1984.

Dwivedi A. N. *T.S. Eliot: A Critical*, New Delhi: Atlantic, 2002.

Eliot Valerie (Ed.). *The Letters of T. S. Eliot, Vol. 1: 1898-1922*. London: Faber & Faber, 1988.

Ellen Mary. *American Poets of the Twentieth Century Notes*, Lincoln. Nebraska: Cliffs Notes, 2000.

Ellmann Richard and O'Clair Robert. *The Norton Anthology of Modern Poetry*, 2nd Ed, New York, London: Norton, 1988. www.wwnorton.com

Eliot Charles William. *The Durable Satisfactions of Life*, New York: Bibliolife, 1910.

Eliot Thomas Stearns. *On Poetry and Poets*, London: Faber and Faber, 1955.

—*Selected Poems*: T.S. Eliot, London: Faber and Faber, 1954.

Feuer Lewis. *What is Alienation: The Career of a Concept in D. Burrows & F.R. Lapides (Eds.) Alienation: A casebook,* New York: Crowell, 1969.

Forbes Deborah. *Sincerity's Shadow: Self-Consciousness in British Romantic and Mid-Twentieth-Century American Poetry,* London: Harvard University Press, 2004.

George. A. G. *T. S. Eliot: his Mind and Art*, 2nd rev. ed. Bombay: Asia Publishing House 1969.

Gillies Marry, Ann and Aurelea, Mahood. *An Introduction: Modernist Literature*, Edinburgh: Edinburgh University Press, 2007.

Gordon Lindall. *Eliot's Early Years*, Oxford: Oxford University Press, 1977.

Grant Michael. *The Critical Heritage: T.S. Eliot*, Vol.1, London and New York: Routledge, 1982.

Harold Bloom. *T.S. Eliot: Comprehensive Research and Study Guide Bloom's Major Poets*, Broomall: Chelsea House Publishers, 1999.

—*Bloom's Literary Themes: Alienation*, New York: InfoBase 2009.

Hargrove Nancy Duvall. *Landscape as a Symbol in the Poetry of T.S. Eliot*, Jackson Miss: University Press of Mississippi, 1978.

Harrison G. B. *Major British Writers*, New York: Harcourt, Brace and World, Inc. 1957.

Hulme T. E. *Lecture on Modern Poetry: Further Speculations*, Minneapolis: University of Minnesota Press, 1955.

J. Scott Stanley *Frontiers of Consciousness: Interdisciplinary Studies in American Philosophy and Poetry*, New York: Fordham University Press, 1999.

Jack, Flam and Deutch, Mirriam, *Primitivism and the Twentieth Century Art* University of California Press, 2003.

Jeffares A. N. and Bushrui, Suheil. *York Notes on Selected Poems*: T.S. Eliot, New York: York Press, 1982.

Jessie L. Weston, *From Ritual to Romance*, Garden City: Doubleday Anchor Books, 1957.

Jones Genesius, *Approach to the Purpose: A Study of the Poetry of T.S. Eliot*, London: Hodder and Stoughton, 1964.

Jr. Miller James. E. *T.S. Eliot: The Making of An American Poet 1888-1922*, Pennsylvania: Pennsylvania University Press, 2005.

Kalaidjian Walter. *The Cambridge Companion to Modernism*, London: Cambridge University Press, 2006.

Kaplan Robert. B. *T.S. Eliot's Major Poems and Plays*, Lincoln, Nebraska: Cliffs Notes, 1997.

Kaplan, Harold. *Poetry, Politics &Culture: Argument in the Work of Eliot, Pound, Stevens & Williams*, New Brunswick, New Jersey: Transaction, 2006.

Kennedy X. J. and Gioia, Dana. *An Introduction to Poetry*, Ninth Ed, New York: Longman, 1988.

Kenner Hugh. *The Invisible Poet: T. S. Eliot*, London: Mathuen and Co. Ltd, 1985.

Kimmelman, Burt. *The Facts on File: Companion to 20th Century American Poetry*, United, States of America: Facts on File, 2005.

Kreizenbeck Alan. *Zoe Akins: Broadway Playwright*. New York :Praeger, 2004.

Laity Cassandra and Gish Nancy. K. *Gender, Desire and Sexuality in T.S. Eliot*, Cambridge: Cambridge University Press, 2004.

Lamos Colleen. *Deviant Modernism*, Cambridge: Cambridge University Press, 2004.

Lawrence Karen, Seifter Betsy and Ratner Lois. *The McGraw-Hill Guide to English Literature: William Blake to D.H. Lawrence*, New York: McGraw-Hill, 1985.

Leavell, Linda. *Eliot's Ritual Method: Ash Wednesday T.S. Eliot: Essays from the Southern Review*. Ed. James Olney, Oxford: Clarendon Press, 1988.

Leavis F.R, *New Bearings of English Poetry*, London: Chatto and Windus, 1961.

Lehman David. *The Oxford Book of American Poetry*, Oxford: Oxford University Press, 2006.

Levenson Michael. *The Cambridge Companion to Modernism*, Cambridge: Cambridge University Press, 1999.

Matheikal Tomichan. *English Poetry: from John Donne to Ted Hughes*, New Delhi: Atlantic Publishers, 2007.

McDiarmid Laurie. J. *T.S. Eliot's Civilized Savage: religious Eroticism and Poetics,* Vol.22. New York and London: Routledge, 2003.

McGowan Christopher. J. *Blackwell Guides to Literature: Twentieth Century American Literature*, Oxford: Blackwell, 2004.

McIntire Gabrielle. *Modernism, Memory, and Desire: T. S. Eliot and Virginia Woolf,* Cambridge: Cambridge University Press, 2008.

Mackillop Ian and Storer Richard. *F.R. Leavis: Essays and Documents*, Sheffield: Sheffield Academic Press, 1995.

McDonald Peter. *Serious Poetry: Form and Authority from Yeats to Hill*, Oxford: Clarendon Press, 2002.

Miller Marlowe. A. *Masterpieces of British Literature*, London: Greenwood Press, 2006.

Milne Ira Mark and Kelly David. Poetry for Students, Vol 9, Detroit and New York: Gale Group, 2000.

Mishra, B. M. *The Poetry of T. S. Eliot,* New Delhi: Atlantic Publishers, 2003.

Moody Anthony David. *The Cambridge Companion to T.S. Eliot,* Cambridge: Cambridge University Press, 1994.

Morrison, Paul. *The Poetics of Fascism: Ezra, Pound, T.S. Eliot and Paul, De Man*, New York Oxford: Oxford University Press, 1996.

Murphy, Russell, Elliott. *Critical Companion to T.S. Eliot, A literary Reference to his Life and Work*, Untied States of America: InfoBase, 2007.

Myers Jack and Wojahan David. *A Profile of Twentieth-Century American Poetry*, Illinois: Southern Illinois University Press, 1991.

North Michael. *The Dialect of Modernism, Race, Language and Twentieth-Century Literature*, New York: Oxford University Press, 1994.

North Michael. *A Norton Critical Edition*: T.S. Eliot, The Waste Land, Los Angels: W. W. Norton & Company, Inc. 2001. www. wwnorton.com

Olson Liesl. *Modernism and the Ordinary*, Oxford New York: Oxford University Press, 2009.

O'Neil Michael. *The All—Sustaining Air: Romantic Legacies and Renewals in British, American and Irish poetry since 1900*, United States: Oxford University Press, 2007.

Oser Lee. *The Ethics of Modernism, Moral Ideas in Yeats Eliot, Joyce, Woolf and Beckett*, New York: Cambridge University Press, 2007.

Palmer Marja. *Men and Women in T.S. Eliot's Early Poetry*, Lund: Lund University Press, 1996.

Patterson, Anita. *Race, American Literature and Transitional Modernisms*, Cambridge, New York: Cambridge University Press, 2008.

Paul Lauter. *Heath Anthology of American Literature*, Houghton Mifflin, Vol, A, Ed, 5th, 2005.

Perloff Marjorie. *Differentials: Poetry, Poetics, and Pedagogy*, New York: The University of Alabama Press, 2004.

Raffel Burton. *T.S. Eliot*, New York: Frederick Ungar, 1982.

Rainey Lawrence. *The Annotated Waste Land with Eliot's Contemporary Prose*, Second Ed, New Haven & London: Yale University Press, 2006.

Raghavan Thattarathodi. *Intellectual Romantics: A Study in Modern English Poetry*, New Delhi: Atlantic Publishers, 1994.

Rajan Balachandra. *The Overwhelming Question: A Study of the Poetry of T.S. Eliot*, Toronto: University of Toronto Press, 1976.

Rampal Dushiant Kumar. *Poetic Theory and Practice of T.S. Eliot*, New Delhi: Atlantic, 1996.

Rao Yeshodhara Gopala. *T.S. Eliot and the romantic Poets*, New Delhi: Atlantic Publishers, 1996.

Roberts Beth Ellen. *One voice and many: modern poets in dialogue*, Massachusetts: Rosemont Publishing, 2006.

Roberts, Neil. *A Companion to Twentieth-Century Poetry*, Oxford: Blackwell, 2001.

Rosen David. *Maturity and Poetic Style*, ProQuest Direct Complete. Raritan; (Spring, 2005): p.88.

Rozakis Laurie. E. *The Complete Idiot's Guide to American Literature*, New York: Alpha books, 1999.

Sanders Andrew. *The Short Oxford History of English Literature*, 2nd Edit London: Durham, 1999.

Sarker Sunil Kumar. *T.S. Eliot: Poetry, Plays and Prose*, New Delhi: Atlantic, 2008.

Shucard Alan, Moramarco Fred and Sullivan William. *Modern American Poetry: 1865-1950*, Massachusetts: The University of Massachusetts Press, 1989.

Schmidt Michael. *A Reader's Guide to Fifty Modern British Poets*, London and New York: Heinemann and Barnes & Noble, 1979.

Scofield Martin. *T. S. Eliot: The Poems*, London: Faber and Faber, 1994.

Sigg Eric. *The American T. S. Eliot*, New York: Cambridge University Press, 1989.

Singh Naorem Khagendra. *T.S. Eliot: A Reconsideration*, New Delhi: A.P.H. Publishing Corporation, 2001.

Singh Rajni. *Tennyson and T.S. Eliot: A Comparative Study*, New Delhi: Sarup and Sons, 2005.

Smidt Kristian. *POETRY and Belief in the Work OF T.S ELIOT*, New York: The Humanities Press, 1961.

Spanos, William V. *Repetition in The Waste Land: A Phenomenological De-Struction. Boundary 2: An International Journal of Literature and Culture* 7.3 (1979): 225-85.

Stead, C. K. *The New Poetic: Yeats to Eliot*, London: Hutchinson, 1964.

Stephen Martin. *An Introductory Guide to English Literature*, Longman: York Press, 1984.

Sullivan Sheila. *Critics on T.S. Eliot*, London: George Allen and Unwin, 1973.

Thomas Parkinson, *W.B. Yeats, Self-Critic: A Study of His Early Verse*, Berkeley: University of California Press, 1951.

Tiwari Nidhi. *Imagery and Symbolism in T.S. Eliot's Poetry*, New Delhi: Atlantic, 2001.

Traversi Derek. *T. S. Eliot: The Longer Poems*, New York: Harcourt Brance Jovanovich, 1976.

Thornley G. C and Roberts, Gwyneth. *An Outline of English Literature*, Edinburgh: Longman, 1968.

Thorne Sara. *Mastering Poetry*, New York: Palgrave Macmillan, 2006.

Unger Leonard. *University of Minnesota Pamphlets on American Writers: T.S. Eliot*, No.8. Minneapolis: University of Minnesota Press, 1961.

Wadikar Shailaja. B. *Vijay Tendulkar: A Pioneer Playwright*, New Delhi: Atlantic, 2008.

Walsh George. *50 Plus One Great Books You Should Have Read: And Probably Didn't*, Chicago: Encouragement Press, 2007.

Ward David. *T.S. Eliot between Two Worlds: A Reading of T.S. Eliot's Poetry and Plays*, London: Routledge & Kegan Paul, 1973.

Ward John Powell. *The Spell of the Song: Letters, Meaning and English Poetry*, Madison, Teaneck: Fairleigh, Dickinson, University Press, 2004.

Williamson George. *A Reader's Guide to T.S. Eliot: a poem-by-poem-analysis*, New York: The Noonday Press, 1953.